The Marxism of Che Guevara

The Marxism of Che Guevara

Philosophy, economics, and revolutionary warfare

by Michael Lowy

Translated by Brian Pearce

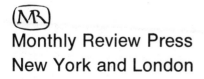
Monthly Review Press
New York and London

Originally published as La pensée de Che Guevara,
by François Maspero, Paris, France, copyright © 1970
by Librairie François Maspero

Library of Congress Cataloging in Publication Data
Lowy, Michael.
   The Marxism of Che Guevara.
   Translation of La Pensée de ''Che'' Guevara.
   Bibliography: p.
   1. Guevara, Ernesto, 1928-1967. 2. Communism —
1945-   I: Title.
F2849.22.G85L6   335.43   72-92030
ISBN 0-85345-274-1

Monthly Review Press
62 West 14th Street, New York, N.Y. 10011
47 Red Lion Street, London WCIR 4PF

Manufactured in the United States of America

10 9 8 7 6 5 4 3 2

Contents

Introduction: Che's theoretical contribution   7

Part I: Che's philosophy
1. Che and Marxism   11
2. The revolution is made by men   19
3. The new man   25
4. Humanist values   29

Part II: Che's economic ideas
Introduction   35
1. Productive forces and production relations   39
2. The law of value and socialist planning   45
3. The budgetary system of finance   54
4. Material and moral incentives   59
5. Voluntary labor and communism   70

Part III: Revolutionary warfare
Introduction   75
1. Sociology of the revolution   78
2. Guerrilla warfare   86
3. The general strike   100
4. The world revolution   106

Part IV: Guevarism today   113

Appendix: Che's reading   119

Bibliography   125

Introduction:
Che's theoretical contribution

Several lives of Che have already been written, but as yet no thorough analysis of his ideas has appeared. His life was certainly a quite remarkable one: from the asthmatic medical student in Buenos Aires to the guerrilla commander, from the fighter in the Sierra Maestra to the chairman of the National Bank of Cuba, and, finally, from the Minister of Industries to the *guerrillero* hunted down and killed in Bolivia through the efforts of the CIA. It was a vivid, meteoric, exemplary life—the life of a man whom Sartre described as "the most complete man of his time," one who can easily be compared to the giants of the Renaissance for the stupendous many-sidedness of his personality: doctor and economist, revolutionary and banker, military theoretician and ambassador, deep political thinker and popular agitator, able to wield the pen and the submachine gun with equal skill. The extraordinary character of this life, without precedent in the history of the twentieth century, accounts for and illuminates the rise of the Che myth: Che the romantic adventurer, the Red Robin Hood, the Don Quixote of communism, the new Garibaldi, the Marxist Saint-Just, the Cid Campeador of the wretched of the earth, the Sir Galahad of the beggars, the secular Christ, the San Ernesto de la Higuera revered by the Bolivian peasants, the Bolshevik devil-with-a-knife-between-his-teeth who haunts the dreams of the rich, the "red pyromaniac" (*Der Spiegel*) kindling braziers of subversion all over the world, and so on.

Behind this mythic and romantic appearance, however (an appearance of which Guevara was aware and with which he played ironically, comparing himself to Don Quixote in his last letter to his family), is hidden something more profound that illuminates Che's life and gives it its true meaning: *the rigorous, total, and monolithic coherence between theory and practice, words and deeds.* Only in the light of this coherence can one understand Che's decision—a surprising one, hard to reconcile with the usual concept of a "politician" and "statesman"—to give up his ministerial office in Cuba for the Bolivian *maquis,* in order to carry out a precisely defined political task: to break down the isolation of the Cuban Revolution and open a second front to help Vietnam.

Though the sensationalist press, the dominant ideological system, may try to "retrieve" the myth of the heroic adventurer, it cannot "digest" the consistent revolutionary militant who put his ideas into practice. Che's heroism was no abstraction, but heroism in the service of a cause, an idea, the socialist revolution as he understood it. "When we think of Che, we do not think fundamentally of his military virtues. No! Warfare is a means and not an end; warfare is a tool of revolutionaries. The important thing is the revolution; the important thing is the revolutionary cause, revolutionary ideas, revolutionary objectives, revolutionary sentiments, revolutionary virtues."[1] Che's revolutionary ideas are thus not "retrievable," and cannot be transformed into harmless articles of consumption. On the contrary, they constitute a precious heritage whose richness and importance have been appreciated by rebellious youth not only in Latin America but in every continent. As Fidel Castro said in a tribute to Che: "Che's writings, Che's political and revolutionary thinking, will be of permanent value in the Cuban revolutionary process and in the Latin American revolutionary process. And we do not doubt that his ideas, as a man of action, as a man of thought, as a man of untarnished moral virtues, as a man of unexcelled human sensitivity, as a man of spotless conduct, have and will continue to have universal value."[2] His is a theoretical legacy which, like those bequeathed by Marx, Engels, Lenin, Trotsky, Luxemburg, and Gramsci, contributes not merely to the interpreting of the world but also to changing it.

It is therefore necessary and urgent to suggest the initial outlines of a systematic study of Che's thought, which is both orthodox Marxist and at the same time fiercely anti-dogmatic; rooted in the fertile soil of the Cuban Revolution and yet bearing a universal message; deeply realistic and yet animated by a powerful prophetic inspiration; scrupulously attentive to the concrete technical problems of financial administration or military tactics, but at the same time preoccupied with the philosophical questions implicit in the communist future; severe, inflexible, intolerant, irreconcilable on the plane of principle, but flexible, versatile, and capable of delicate variation as regards forms of application to a complex and changing reality.

The aim of my book is to show that Guevara's ideas constitute a coherent whole, and are built on the basic premises of Marxism-Leninism, their philosophical, humanistic, ethical, economic, sociological, political, and military themes all closely linked together. I also wish to show the relation between Che's ideas and those of Marx and the different Marxist trends of our time, emphasizing the way in which Che's ideas seem to me to transcend Stalinism and reformism, and to go back to the living sources of revolutionary communism. Finally, I shall try to show how these ideas furnish an original and stimulating theoretical contribution to Marxist thought, especially as regards three major problems: (1) the human significance of communism, (2) the political economy of regimes in transition to socialism, and (3) the politico-military strategy of the revolution in the Third World.[3]

Notes

[*Note:* For convenience' sake, shortened versions of the titles of the two collections of Guevara's works in English will be used throughout the notes. *Venceremos! The Speeches and Writings of Che Guevara* will be referred to as *Venceremos;* and *Che: Selected Works of Ernesto Che Guevara* will be referred to as *Selected Works.* Shortened versions of speech and article titles will be used after the first appearance. Full biographical information for every title is in the Bibliography.—Trans.

1. Fidel Castro, "In Tribute to Che," in Che Guevara, *Reminiscences of the Cuban Revolutionary War,* pp. 20–21.
2. Ibid., p. 23.
3. This list is not at all exhaustive. Che's thinking also includes significant contributions on questions which I have not been able to deal with in this book: the struggle against bureaucracy, the economic significance of imperialism, the strictly military tactics of guerrilla warfare, industrialization in Cuba, the role of the party and of cadres in the building of socialism, etc.

Part I: Che's Philosophy

1. Che and Marxism

Che's road to Marxism

"It was concluded that Guevara was one of the international agents of Communism who work underground and who are known to very few others," according to *U.S. News and World Report* (November 9, 1959), quoting "well-informed sources in Guatemala." The myth of Che the Communist agent infiltrated into Cuba, which was spread by the American press after the victory of the *guerrilleros* in 1959, was merely a hateful caricature of an important fact—that Che became a Marxist much sooner than most of the leaders of the Cuban Revolution.[1]

It is possible to establish fairly exactly the time and place of Che's "discovery" of Marxism. It was in Guatemala in 1954, and occurred under the twofold influence of his wife Hilda Gadea, who belonged to the left wing of the Alianza Popular Revolucionaria Americana (Aprista), the revolutionary Peruvian party, and of the Alliance of Democratic Youth, the mass organization linked to the Guatemalan Labor Party, which Che had joined. It was in Hilda's library and that of the Alliance that he made his first acquaintance with the writings of Marx and Lenin.[2]

According to the testimony of the Cuban Mario Dalmau, who knew him in Guatemala at this time, Che had already read "a whole Marxist library" and possessed "a very clear Marxist way of thinking."[3] Obviously, this discovery of Marxism was no mere intellectual and bookish affair for Che, but was the result of a very concrete experience he had undergone, his experience of the poverty

11

and oppression of the Latin American masses, which he came to know during his travels about the rural areas of the continent.[4] On the other hand, it is probable that the Marxist-Leninist formation of his thought was definitively crystallized by that revealing event which was to leave its mark on a whole generation of Latin Americans: the invasion of Guatemala by the mercenaries of Castillo Armas in 1954. Carlos María Gutiérrez has written that Castillo Armas was Che's "negative teacher." The counter-revolution in Guatemala was indeed directly and personally experienced by Che (who even tried, in vain, to organize armed groups to resist the invaders), and it showed him, "didactically," the role played by the big monopolies (United Fruit), American imperialism (John Foster Dulles), the Guatemalan army, Arbenz's pacifism, and so on. We can find other examples of the kind of Marxist radicalization, together with a determination to turn to armed struggle, which Che experienced after the fall of Arbenz, among the intelligentsia and political cadres of Latin American countries that suffered similar events: in Brazil after the fall of Goulart, in the Dominican Republic after the American invasion of 1965, etc.

In Mexico, where he went after the triumph of the counter-revolutionaries in Guatemala, Guevara pursued and deepened his Marxist studies. When he met the Cuban refugees of the 26th of July Movement, Che endeavored to get them to share his knowledge: a Cuban militant, Dario López, who knew him in that period, tells us that it was Che who selected the Marxist works for the library the police found in the training camp of the 26th of July Movement in Mexico, the library that was used for their political instruction courses.

Thus, unlike most of the Cuban leaders, Che did not arrive at Marxism through the experience of the Cuban Revolution itself. On the contrary, he tried, very early on, to interpret this revolution by reference to Marxism. And it was because he was already a Marxist that he was the first to grasp fully the historico-social significance of the Cuban Revolution, proclaiming as early as July 1960 that the revolution had "discovered by its own methods the path that Marx pointed out."[5]

Che's antidogmatic Marxism

One of the essential qualities of Che's Marxism is its passionately antidogmatic character. For Che, Marx was the founder of a new science which can and must develop as a result of the transformation of reality. It is in this sense, in my opinion, that one should interpret the somewhat surprising comparison he makes in his "Notes for the Study of the Ideology of the Cuban Revolution" (1960) between Marx and Newton.[6] For Che, Marx was not a Pope endowed by the Holy Ghost with the gift of infallibility; nor were his writings Tablets of the Law graciously handed down on Mount Sinai. In this same passage Che stresses that Marx, although an intellectual giant, had committed mistakes which could and should be criticized: as regards Latin America, for example, his interpretation of Bolívar, or the analysis of the Mexicans he made with Engels, in which he "gave some race and nationality theories as fact which are inadmissible today."[7]

Guevara complained on a number of occasions about "the scholasticism that has held back the development of Marxist philosophy" and has even systematically hindered study of the period of the building of socialism. Against this scholasticism (he obviously has Stalinism in mind) and against every tendency to solidify Marxism into a grand system of eternal truths, unchanging and unchangeable, offered for pious contemplation to the faithful, Che used the same argument that Lenin used against the petrified

orthodoxy of the Second International: it must not be
forgotten that Marxism ought, in the last analysis, to serve
as a guide to action.[8]

We thus find in Guevara an acute awareness of the need
for the creative development of Marxism-Leninism, above
all in relation to the new problems presented by transitional societies, for which the writings of Marx and Lenin
furnish only an introduction—precious and necessary, to
be sure, but insufficient. This does not in the least mean
that Che's thinking was not orthodox, in the true sense of
the word, that is, formed on the basis of the fundamental
principles of revolutionary Marxism and the dialectical
materialist method.

The antidogmatism which is characteristic of Che's
thinking from the methodological standpoint is reflected
in his economic and political views, enabling them to transcend the limitations "systematically" imposed by the
Stalinist bureaucracy.[9] Without losing our sense of proportion, we can say that Che carried out, at least as far as
Latin America is concerned, the same task of revolutionary
renovation with regard to the solidified "Marxism" of the
official left that Lenin carried out with regard to the
"Marxist" social-democracy of the Second International.

Marxist humanism

For Che, genuine Marxism does not exclude humanism:
it incorporates it as one of the necessary elements in its
own world outlook. It is as a humanist that Che stresses
the originality and importance of the Cuban Revolution,
which has sought to build "a Marxist, socialist system
which is coherent, or nearly so, in which man is placed at
the center, and in which the individual, the human personality, with the importance it holds as an essential factor in
the revolution, is taken into account."[10]

We know that in 1959 Fidel defined the Cuban Revolution as a *humanist* revolution. With the transition (the "growing-across") of the revolution to socialism, and with Fidel's adherence to Marxism-Leninism (1960–1961), this humanism was not simply abolished; it was negated-conserved-transcended (*Aufhebung*) by the new Marxist humanism of the Cuban revolutionaries. In a speech in 1961, Fidel explicitly stressed the humanistic inspiration of the thinking of Marx and Lenin: "Who has said that Marxism is the renunciation of human sentiments . . . ? It was precisely love for man which conceived Marxism, it was love for man, for humanity, the desire to combat misery, injustice, and all the exploitation suffered by the proletariat which made Marxism rise from the mind of Karl Marx when precisely Marxism could arise, when precisely a real possibility and more than a real possibility could arise—that historical necessity of a social revolution of which Karl Marx was the interpreter. But what could this interpreter have been but for the wealth of human sentiment of men like him, like Engels, like Lenin?"[11]

To Che, this passage in Fidel's speech was absolutely essential, and he recommended every militant of the Cuban party engrave it in his memory as "the most efficient weapon against all deviations."[12]

During 1963 and 1964 Che discovered the writings of the young Marx. It was probably the great economic debate that began in Cuba at that time that prompted him to read the *Economic and Philosophical Manuscripts of 1844*. While recognizing the theoretical limitations of the young Marx—whose language "shows the influence of the philosophic ideas that had contributed to his development" and whose economic ideas were "very imprecise," not yet having acquired the scientific rigor of *Capital*—Che emphasized the interest of these writings, which deal with the problems of the liberation of man as a social being, with communism as the solution of the contradictions that bring about man's alienation.[13]

And what about *Capital?* Is it not, in contrast to the writings of the young Marx, "purely scientific" and even "antihumanist"? This neopositivist view of *Capital,* which was very widespread in the period of the Second International and has reappeared in a new form in our day, overlooks the fact that the denunciation of the inhumanity of capitalism—with the possibility of its being transcended by a society in which *men* rationally control *things*—is one of the crucial themes of Marx's principal work, a theme that does not contradict its scientific character but, on the contrary, is dialectically connected with it. Guevara, however, fully grasped the humanist dimension of *Capital,* as well as the reasons why this dimension is not always "visible" to the uninformed reader: "The weight of this monument of the human mind is such that it has made us frequently forget the humanist character (in the best sense of the word) of what it is concerned with. The mechanism of production relations and their consequence, the class struggle, hides, to some extent, the objective fact that it is men who are the actors in history."[14]

"Humanist in the best sense of the word": by using this expression Che suggests that it is vital to distinguish between Marx's humanism and humanism "in the bad sense of the word": bourgeois humanism, traditional Christian humanism, philanthropic humanism, and so forth. Against every abstract humanism that claims to be "above classes" (and which, in the last analysis, is bourgeois), Che's humanism, like that of Marx, is explicitly involved in a proletarian class outlook. It is thus radically opposed to "bad humanism" by virtue of this fundamental premise: the liberation of man and the realization of his potentialities can be accomplished only through the *proletarian revolution* which abolishes the exploitation of man by man and establishes men's rational domination over their process of social life. In his conception of humanism it is possible and even probable that Che was influenced by the

work of the Argentinian thinker Aníbal Ponce (1898–
1938), one of the pioneers of Marxism in Latin America,
whose book *Humanismo burgués y humanismo proletario*
(1935) was rightly reissued in Cuba in 1962. Ponce shows
the fundamental contrast between the humanism of the
bourgeoisie and that of the working people and emphasizes
that the "new man," the "complete man," the person who
unites theory and practice, culture and labor, can be
brought about only through the coming to power of the
proletariat.[15] The Marxist humanism of Che is thus, above
all, a *revolutionary* humanism which finds expression in his
conception of the role of men in the revolution, in his
communist ethics, and in his vision of the new man.

Notes

1. Fidel Castro generously acknowledged this in an interview he
   gave in 1965: "I believe that at the time I met Che Guevara he
   had a greater revolutionary development, ideologically speaking, than I had. From the theoretical point of view he was
   more formed, he was a more advanced revolutionary than I
   was." (Quoted in Lee Lockwood, *Castro's Cuba, Cuba's Fidel,*
   p. 162.)

2. Apparently Che entertained some reservations about the Partido
   Guatemalteco de Trabajo (PGT), whose bureaucratic sectarian-
   ism displeased him. According to a well-known story told by
   his old friend Ricardo Rojo (a somewhat dubious source), the
   Guatemalan Minister of Health declined to give Che a job as a
   doctor because he did not hold a party card. "Look, friend,"
   Che replied, "the day I decide to affiliate myself, I'll do it
   from conviction, not through obligation, understand?" (Rojo,
   My Friend Che, p. 56.) As for the left wing of Aprista, which
   Che had also encountered during his stay in Peru in 1953, it is
   interesting to note that in the 1960s it became the MIR (Movi-
   miento de Izquierda Revolucionaria), led by Luis de la Puente
   Uceda, and was one of the first organizations of the communist "New Left" in Latin America.

3. *Granma* (French edition), October 29, 1967.

4. "Because of the circumstances in which I traveled ... I came into close contact with poverty, hunger, and disease; with the inability to treat a child because of lack of money; with the stupefaction provoked by continual hunger and punishment ..." (Speech of August 19, 1960, *Venceremos*, p. 112.) Che's approach can be compared to the tradition of the "Red doctors" of nineteenth-century Europe, who (especially in Germany) were drawn toward doctrines of social revolution as a result of their experiences in medical practice.

5. Speech to the First Congress of Latin American Youth, July 28, 1960, *Selected Works*, p. 247.

6. "One should be a 'Marxist' as naturally as one is a 'Newtonian' in physics, or a 'Pasteurian' in biology, considering that if new facts determine new concepts, these new concepts will never take away that part of truth which the older concept had." (*Selected Works*, p. 49.)

7. Ibid.

8. See "Socialism and Man in Cuba" (1965), *Selected Works*, pp. 115–69; and "On Party Militancy" (1963), *Venceremos*, p. 244.

9. Che was aware, moreover, of the connection between dogmatism and bureaucracy. In a passage alluding to the "Escalante affair," he wrote in April 1962: "There had appeared throughout the country, as a baneful vice that it was necessary for us to eliminate completely, aloofness from the masses, dogmatism, sectarianism. Because of them, we were threatened by bureaucratism." ("With the Workers of the CTC," *Oeuvres III: Textes politiques*, p. 89.)

10. Guevara, "Il piano e gli uomini," *Il Manifesto*, no. 7 (December 1969), p. 36 (a verbatim record of conversations held in 1964 at the Ministry for Industries).

11. Quoted in "The Role of the Marxist-Leninist Party" (1963), *Selected Works*, pp. 109–10.

12. Ibid., p. 110.

13. "On the Budgetary System of Finance" (1964), ibid., pp. 112–13 (translation modified).

14. Ibid., p. 113 (translation modified).

15. Cf. A. Ponce, *Humanismo burgués y humanismo proletario*, p. 113.

2. The revolution is made by men

For Che, Marxism was first and foremost the philosophy of praxis, the theory of revolutionary action. As he saw it, Marx represented a qualitative change in the history of social thought, not only because he contributed a scientific interpretation of history, but also and above all because he introduced a profoundly revolutionary idea: it is not enough to interpret the world, we have to change it.[1]

It is well known that in the economistic Marxism of the Second International, the problematic of revolutionary initiative tended to disappear in favor of that of "the iron laws which determine the inevitable transformation of the world." Karl Kautsky summed up this view of history in his memorable statement: "The Socialist Party is a revolutionary party; it is not a party that makes revolutions. We know that our aims can be realized only through a revolution, but we also know that it is not in our power to make a revolution, any more than it is in the power of our opponents to prevent it. We have therefore never thought of promoting or preparing a revolution."[2] Lenin, in contrast, from his earliest polemics with the Russian "economists" in 1902 and with Plekhanov during the Revolution of 1905, emphasized the role played by the historical initiative of the vanguard and the masses in the revolution.

In Latin America, where the majority of the traditional Communist parties are sunk in Menshevism, Che's ideas undoubtedly represented a return to the living sources of Leninism. Lenin, wrote Che, teaches us that "the transition from one society to another cannot be mechanical," that the conditions for it can be accelerated by certain catalysts. In 1917 revolutionary Leninism meant—as it means in Latin America today—that: "If there were a vanguard of the proletariat capable of enunciating the fundamental demands of the proletariat, of having a clear idea of what direction to take, and of trying to seize power so as to establish the new society, headway could be made and intermediate stages could be skipped."[3] This means that historical materialism, as Che saw it, does not conceive of history as being "mechanically determined by an accumulation of economic forces." A revolutionary transformation always implies the "overwhelming of one social class by another, from the political and historical standpoint." In other words, "one can never separate economic analysis from the historical fact of the class struggle," and this means, further, that one can never leave out of account "man, who is the living expression of the class struggle."[4]

Against the neo-Kautskian waiting attitude of those parties of the traditional left which refused to act on the pretext that "conditions are not yet mature," Che stressed that the Marxist parties cannot "await with folded arms" the emergence of all the objective and subjective conditions necessary for "power to fall into the people's hands like a ripe fruit." Starting from the experience of the guerrilla war in Cuba—which by its very action had created one of the subjective conditions for the revolution, namely, certainty that a change was possible—he formulated this general principle of the theory of revolutionary praxis: the role of the vanguard parties is to contribute to creating the conditions needed for the seizure of power, "and not to await a revolutionary wave that will appear from the masses."[5] It is on the basis of these premises that Castro's and Guevara's theory of the guerrilla nucleus as catalyst has to be understood. I shall come back to this point.

This does not mean that Che tended toward a purely voluntarist view of revolution. He was fully aware that it is the internal contradictions of an economic and social formation that create the objective conditions necessary for the coming of a "revolutionary situation." But he was also aware that without the conscious action of the vanguard, and, consequently, of the masses, the revolution cannot take place. Thus, analyzing Cuba's transition to socialism, Guevara observed that the vanguard had "hastened the course of events," but then immediately acknowledged that it had done this "within the limits of what is objectively possible."[6] This conception, which transcends both the economistic fatalism inspired by the metaphysical materialism of the eighteenth century ("circumstances shape men") *and* idealist-voluntarist subjectivism, is precisely that of Marx himself when he wrote in *The Eighteenth Brumaire of Louis Bonaparte* that men make their own history—not arbitrarily, but under given conditions. It is in this sense that we have to interpret Che's famous slogan: "The duty of a revolutionary is to make revolution," which is not at all a tautology (it is enough to compare it with Kautsky's statement, quoted above), but rather proves an adequate understanding of a fundamental principle of historical materialism: "Human history differs from natural history in this, that we have made the former but not the latter."[7] Or, as Guevara writes, the mechanism of the relations of production must not hide the objective fact that "it is men who are the actors in history."

While men have always been the actors in history, it is only with the socialist revolution that they begin to play this role consciously. The historical specificity of the proletarian revolution—not as a single act but as a permanent process leading from the struggle for power to the establishment of communism—is that it is for the first time a fully conscious human undertaking. "After the October Revolution of 1917 . . . man acquired a new consciousness. The men of the French Revolution, who gave so many beautiful things to mankind . . . were, however, simple instruments of history . . . They were not yet able to direct history, to construct their own history consciously. After the October Revolution this was achieved . . ."[8]

This means that, unlike the great social transformations of the past, "Communism is a goal of humanity that is reached consciously."[9] This theme constitutes one of the richest and most significant contributions made by Che to the development of Marxist humanism. He takes as his point of departure a phrase of Marx's in the *Economic and Philosophical Manuscripts of 1844:* "[Communism] is the solution of the riddle of history, and it knows itself to be this solution." Che interprets this somewhat ambiguous statement in terms of his own conception of communism: "Marx thought about man's liberation and considered communism the solution to the contradictions that produced man's alienation, but he considered that solution a conscious act . . . Man is the conscious actor of history. Without the *consciousness* which encompasses his awareness as a social being there can be no communism."[10]

The concrete politico-economic expression of this principle in a society in transition is the plan, the instrument by which man's consciousness directs economic and social development toward communism. Che's economic thinking is therefore rigorously coherent with his general theory of the genesis of communism. I shall come back to this point. (This is also a theme in the previously mentioned book by Aníbal Ponce, which Che probably read some time in 1962 or 1963: "Man as a conscious factor in evolution; man transforming nature and society in accordance with a carefully worked-out plan; man who has ceased to be a slave, whether submissive or desperate, in order to become the absolute master of his powers: this is Soviet man, who brings his will into what had seemed inaccessible to it . . . By socializing the instruments of production and breaking down forever the barriers that stood in the way of the free development of social forces, the proletariat, for the first time in the

world, begins to trace out the history of man in full awareness of what it wants and what it is doing. "[11])

It is not, of course, a matter of the conscious action of a
leader or of a vanguard alone: the communist society of
the future is not a Christmas present from an omniscient
and far-seeing Father of the Peoples, or from an elite of
wise and virtuous citizens. It is the people themselves who
must "really become the creator and leader of their history, where their own happiness will be built by their own
hands." Che's political thought, like that of Marx and
Lenin, is built around this fundamental principle of all
truly revolutionary theory: *the emancipation of the working people will be the task of the working people themselves.* This is why Che, while acknowledging the imperfec-
tion of Cuba's revolutionary institutions, stressed the great
importance of the fact that in Cuba "the masses now make
history as a conscious aggregate of individuals who struggle
for the same cause"; that the Cuban people are "individuals who have achieved the awareness of what must
be done, men who struggle to leave the domain of necessity and enter that of freedom."[12] This was likewise
Lenin's idea when he wrote, in April 1918: "Such a revolution can be successfully carried out only if the majority of
the population, and primarily the majority of the working
people, engage in independent creative work as makers of
history. Only if the proletariat and the poor peasants dis-
play sufficient class consciousness, devotion to principle,
self-sacrifice and perseverance, will the victory of the
socialist revolution be assured."[13]

Notes

1. "Notes for the Study of the Ideology of the Cuban Revolution"
   (1960), *Selected Works,* p. 50. This is the very first piece of
   writing in which Che presented himself as a Marxist.

2. Karl Kautsky, *Der Weg zur Macht,* p. 57.
3. "On Party Militancy," *Venceremos,* p. 246.
4. "Socialist Planning" (1965), ibid., p. 406 (translation modified).
5. "Marxist-Leninist Party," *Selected Works,* pp. 104–6.
6. "Socialist Planning," *Venceremos,* p. 404.
7. Marx, *Capital,* vol. I, p. 367n (Marx is here quoting Vico).
8. "Volunteer Labor" (speech in January 1964), *Selected Works,* p. 307.
9. "Budgetary System," *Selected Works,* p. 307.
10. Ibid., p. 113. Cf. also Guevara, "La banca, el crédito y el socialismo," *Cuba socialista,* no. 31 (March 1964): "We do not conceive of communism as the mechanical sum of consumer goods in a given society, but as the outcome of a conscious act."
11. Ponce, *Humanismo burgués,* pp. 163, 169.
12. "Volunteer Labor" and "Socialism and Man," *Selected Works,* pp. 310, 162, 168. There is a striking similarity between these views of Che's and the brilliant writings of the young Lukács in the heroic period of the Bolshevik Revolution. In an article entitled *Die Rolle der Moral in der kommunistischen Produktion* (a splendidly Guevarist title!), Lukács stresses that the transition from the reign of necessity to that of freedom "cannot be the outcome of an automatic law of blind social forces, but must result from a free decision by the working class . . . The direction that the development of society will take depends on the consciousness, the spiritual and moral integrity, the power of judgment and the capacity for sacrifice of the proletariat." (*Frühschriften 1919-1922,* pp. 92, 94.)
13. Lenin, "The Immediate Tasks of the Soviet Government," *Works,* vol. 27, p. 241.

3. The new man

The dream of all great revolutionaries, from Rousseau to Lenin, has been to change not merely "the world" but also "man": the revolution, for them, is not only a transformation of social structures, institutions, and regimes, but also a profound, radical, and "overturning" (*umwälzende*) transformation of *men,* of their consciousness, ways, values, and habits, of their social relations. A revolution is authentic only if it can create this "new man." For Rousseau, it was a matter of forming the true citizen, in whom the rational general will dominates the narrow particularism of egoistic passions. (Rousseau's thinking could not, of course, owing to its social content and historical determination, transcend certain limits, in particular as regards the concrete social conditions that could enable men to become "citizens.") In the *Economic and Philosophical Manuscripts* Marx speaks with admiration of the communist workers, the bearers of the future, among whom "the brotherhood of man is no empty phrase," and for whom association, society, has already become an end in itself. This is precisely the determined negation of the "bourgeois" described in *The Jewish Question* (1844): an isolated monad, an egoistic atom, moved exclusively by his petty private interest. Finally, for Lenin, communism will create a new generation of free men who will observe the rules of social life without any need for violence, submission, or coercion.[1]

Guevara's ideas belong to this intellectual line of descent. For him too, the supreme and ultimate task of revolution was to create a new man, a *communist* man, the dialectical negation of the individual of capitalist society, transformed into an alienated "human commodity," or capable of becoming, through the workings of imperialism, a carnivore, "a wolf-man in a wolf-community." Because bourgeois society is based, in the last analysis, on the law of the jungle, success can be attained only through the defeat of others. It is a society in which, objectively, necessarily, inevitably, whatever "goodwill" there may be, Christian or other, man is man's enemy.[2]

The radical transformation of society requires, at the same time, a deepgoing transformation of the mental structures of individuals. How, once power has been won, the bourgeoisie expropriated, and the economic structure changed, are those taints of the old society that still survive in the individual consciousness to be got rid of?

By education, both direct and indirect, by raising the cultural level, by propaganda, by ideological work: "Society as a whole must become a gigantic school." But this education is not and cannot be a purely passive apprenticeship: it must also, and above all, take the form of self-education. In the march toward communism the people must educate themselves.[3] This abolition of the moral and ideological aftereffects of bourgeois society is not an automatic and direct result of the socioeconomic transformations which have been carried out. These transformations are a necessary condition for the abolition, but not a sufficient one. They call for conscious and *specific* intervention at the level of superstructure. Moreover, they are gravely jeopardized if the economic methods of building socialism bear the hallmarks of the former society: the production process must also contribute to the political education of the masses and the coming of the new man.

What are the characteristic features of this new man—communist man, or "twenty-first-century man"? Rejecting utopianism, Che restricts himself to a few general assumptions of a necessarily abstract sort, assumptions based on Cuban reality, where the first prefigurations of this future could already be found in the revolutionaries, the guerrilla fighters, who rivaled each other for the most dangerous assignments, with no other satisfaction than that of duty done ("In the attitude of our fighters, we could glimpse the man of the future"); in the masses of the people themselves, through their courage and sacrifice at the critical moments of the Revolution—the invasion of Playa Girón, the rocket bases crisis of October 1962; in the communist youth, a living example of revolutionary fervor and internationalist spirit.[4] Communist man must necessarily be a man of greater inner resources and a greater sense of responsibility, bound to others by a relationship of real solidarity, of concrete universal brotherhood; he must be a man who recognizes himself in his work and who, once the chains of alienation have been broken, "will achieve total awareness of his social being which is equivalent to his full realization as a human creature."[5] A man whose potentiality is what Marx called in his *Theses on Feuerbach* "socialized humanity"—the transcending of that division effected by bourgeois society between "private" and "public," "particular" and "general" interests, between the "man" and the "citizen," the individual and the community.

Does the problematic of communist man, as we find it in Guevara's works, belong to the ideological universe of romantic utopianism? I do not think so. What is utopian is not envisaging the possibility of a "new man," but rather believing in an eternal and unchanging "human nature." Communism is not at all, for Che, "a utopian system based on man's goodness as a man,"[6] but an objective possibility which he glimpses through the concrete experience of the Cuban Revolution.

The theme of the new man as the ultimate aim, the polestar of the socialist revolution, is the touchstone, the central driving idea, of Che's revolutionary humanism, in the light of which the whole of his political thinking needs to be understood.[7]

Notes

1. Lenin, "The State and Revolution," *Works,* vol. 25, p. 456.
2. "Colonialism Is Doomed" (1964), *Selected Works,* p. 339; "Socialism and Man," ibid., p. 158; "Letter to José Medero Mestre," *Oeuvres III: Textes politiques,* p. 317; "Letter to Hildita" (1967), *Selected Works,* p. 425.
3. "Socialism and Man," *Selected Works,* pp. 159, 160.
4. Ibid., pp. 156, 160; also "On Being a Communist Youth" (1962), *Venceremos,* pp. 217-18.
5. "Revolution and Underdevelopment" (1965), *Selected Works,* pp. 350-51; "Socialism and Man," ibid., pp. 162, 166-67.
6. "On Party Militancy," *Venceremos,* p. 245.
7. "Whether Che is discussing the theory of value, the danger of bureaucratism, the cadres of the revolution, the qualities of the young Communist, the building of the party, this [the new man] is the thread that all his thoughts follow." (R. F. Retamar, Introduction, *Oeuvres I: Textes militaires,* p. 18.)

4. Humanist values

The problem of the theoretical status of moral values in Marxism has always been the subject of a philosophical debate with political implications. The classical case was that of the trends in German social-democracy before 1914: on the one hand, idealistic moralism, abstract, dealing in eternities, "above classes," neo-Kantian by derivation (Bernstein); on the other, scientistic "antimoralism" (Kautsky), with positivist overtones. A recent example of the latter attitude is found in Charles Bettelheim's polemical writings against Che. Rejecting the humanistic and moral problematic (in particular, the theme of alienation) as non-Marxist, Bettelheim bases his argument on a passage in the later Engels, where Engels writes to his disciple Lafargue: "When one is a 'man of science,' one does not have an ideal; one works out scientific results, and when one is a party man to boot, one fights to put them into practice. But when one has an ideal, one cannot be a man of science, for one starts out with preconceptions."[1] Now, this passage—which does not seem to me to represent Marx's thinking—belongs to a wholly natural scientistic and positivist outlook which cannot solve the problem: it is quite obvious that the "party man" does not fight to put "scientific results" into practice unless he regards these results as an ideal. Furthermore, the problematic of alienation is not at all alien to the works of the mature Marx. In *Capital*, for example, he writes: "Capital comes more and more to the fore as a social power, whose agent is the capitalist ... It becomes an alienated (*entfremdete*), independent, social power, which stands opposed to society

29

as an object, and as an object that is the capitalist's source of power."[2] The concept of alienation, which bears an abstract "anthropological" character in the *Economic and Philosophical Manuscripts,* becomes more historicized and concrete in the *Grundrisse* and in *Capital.*[3] The dialectical transcending (*Aufhebung*) of this contradiction was approached by Luxemburg, who both admitted that Marxism implies a humanist morality and emphasized that until communism has been established all morality and all humanism must necessarily bear a *class* character. It is probable, if not certain, that Che was ignorant of the polemics among Social-Democrats before the 1914 war, and of the works of Rosa Luxemburg. But he may have read the writings of José Carlos Mariátegui, the founder of the Peruvian Communist Party and the "great ancestor" of Latin American Marxism, whose works were at that very time being "rediscovered" and republished in Cuba. In a chapter of his book *Defensa del Marxismo* entitled "Ethics and Socialism" (which was also published in the first issue of the journal *Tricontinental*), Mariátegui refutes the thesis that Marxism is anti-ethical and suggests that a true proletarian morality "does not emerge mechanically from economic interests; it is formed in the class struggle, carried on in a heroic frame of mind, with passionate will power."[4] It is in the light of this conception that Che's revolutionary humanism needs to be understood.

What are the ethical values to which Guevara explicitly appeals and which inspire his revolutionary struggle and his ideal of the new man?

The supreme value for any real humanism can only be *humanity* itself: "Human life has meaning only to the degree that, and as long as, it is lived in the service of something infinite. For us, humanity is this something infinite." These words, written in 1927 by the Bolshevik leader Adolf Joffe in his farewell letter to Leon Trotsky, define with exactitude the ethical horizon of the Marxist revolutionary for whom humanity is the universal value, the concrete totality which integrates and transcends the individual and the nation as partial moments (in the philosophical sense), and which is identified, in the last analysis, with the world proletariat. It is in this sense that Che speaks of love for people, love for mankind, generous feelings without which "it is impossible to think of an authentic revolutionary," and the essence of which is clearly expressed in the requirement he formulated for the young Communists: always to feel as one's own the great problems of humanity.[5] This experience does not relate to an abstract, vague "philanthropy," but finds its concrete, political expression in international solidarity among peoples, in proletarian internationalism, which, so long as classes continue to exist, is the only true countenance of "love for mankind." (It should be added that this "love" is not at all the same thing as that of traditional Christianity, since it may well be accompanied by its opposite, hatred, an uncompromising hatred of the enemy: "A people without hatred cannot vanquish a brutal enemy."[6])

Humanity as a value necessarily implies the valorization of human life itself. Indeed Che, the theoretician of revolutionary war, of the liberating violence of armed struggle; Che, who insisted that "the oppressor must be killed mercilessly," and who believed that the revolutionary has to become an "efficient and selective" killing machine,[7] this same Major Guevara always showed profound and genuine respect for human life. It is because he regarded life as a value that he criticized the blind terrorism which strikes down innocent victims; that he called on the guerrilla fighter to treat kindly the defenseless vanquished; that he urged clemency toward captured enemy soldiers, and categorically declared that a "wounded enemy should be treated with care and respect."[8]

After the capture and killing of Che in Bolivia, an American magazine was shameless enough to write that

Che, "who had always advocated that no prisoners be taken," had no grounds for complaint. This is a foul lie. Here is what Che wrote on the subject, in *Guerrilla Warfare:* "Clemency as absolute as possible toward the enemy soldiers who go into the fight performing or believing that they perform a military duty. It is a good policy, so long as there are no considerable bases of operations and invulnerable places, to take no prisoners. Survivors ought to be set free. The wounded should be cared for with all possible resources at the time of the action."[9] Several passages in his *Reminiscences of the Cuban Revolutionary War,* as well as the testimony of fellow fighters, confirm that his actual behavior accorded scrupulously with this standard of revolutionary ethics.[10]

To hold life in profound respect and to be ready to take up arms and, if need be, to kill, is contradictory only in the eyes of Christian or pacifist humanism. For revolutionary humanism, for Che, the people's war is the necessary answer, the only possible answer, of the exploited and oppressed to the crimes and the institutionalized violence of the oppressors: "They themselves impel us to this struggle; there is no alternative other than to prepare it and decide to undertake it . . ."[11]

Furthermore, genuine respect for human life cannot be restricted to concern with physical survival alone. The life of the spirit must be respected no less, if not more, than that of the body: it is necessary to safeguard men's *dignity.* This word, which constantly recurs in the writings of Che, Fidel, and other Cuban revolutionaries, has many meanings, but is bound up especially with the idea of *justice.* There is a sentence of José Martí's that Che was very fond of, which he often quoted in his speeches, and in which he saw "the standard of dignity": "A real man should feel on his own cheek the blow inflicted on any other man's." The theme of dignity doubtless has deep roots in Spanish-American civilization. ("*La dignidad,* in

Latin America, is meaningless in the reality of a life that is too wretched, and this is why the word is so loaded with hope that it sets off popular insurrections and gives the signal for revolutions."[12]) And this saying of Martí's immediately makes one think of *Don Quixote,* a work that Che read in the Sierra Maestra during the "literature courses" he gave to peasant recruits in the guerrilla army, and whose hero he ironically identified with in his last letter to his family. (*Don Quixote* was, moreover, the first book that the Cuban revolutionaries had the National Publishing Institute issue "on a mass scale" after they took power in 1959.) It would, however, be a mistake to regard the theme of dignity as alien to Marxism. Did not Marx himself write: "The proletariat . . . needs its courage, its self-respect, its pride, and its sense of independence even more than its bread"?[13]

The problematic of dignity also implies that other value to which Che appeals: *freedom,* which obviously possessed for him, as a Marxist, a meaning quite different from the one ascribed to it by individualistic bourgeois humanism. For Marx, freedom was not the "free play" of individuals confronting each other on the market, but was rational control of nature and social life by men themselves. And this implies precisely the abolition of the "free market" and of every form of alienation—that is, of the domination of men by their own works, and in particular by the production process. This conception of freedom is also that held by Che, for whom the liberation of man presupposes, concretely, "the solution to the contradictions that produced man's alienation." This is why Che does not shrink from declaring that the most important of revolutionary ambitions is to see man liberated from his alienation, that is, first and foremost, from domination by the blind laws of capitalism, the emancipation from which marks man's first step toward the realm of freedom. For Che, the liberation of man is not a single act but a process: freedom must be *built.* In Cuba "the skeleton of our freedom is formed," but its complete accomplishment will not be achieved until the coming of communist society on a world scale.[14]

Humanity, justice, dignity, freedom: these "classical" values gain a new meaning in the revolutionary humanism of Che, because they are envisaged from the standpoint of the proletariat, of the class struggle, of the socialist revolution.

Notes

1. Letter from Engels to Lafargue of August 11, 1884, quoted in Charles Bettelheim, *La Transition vers l'économie socialiste,* p. 170.
2. Marx, *Capital,* vol. III, p. 259.
3. On this, see Ernest Mandel, *The Formation of the Economic Thought of Karl Marx,* ch. 10.
4. *Tricontinental* (English edition), no. 3 (1967), pp. 21–22.
5. "Socialism and Man," *Selected Works,* p. 167; "On Being a Communist Youth," *Venceremos,* p. 218.
6. "Message to the Tricontinental" (1967), *Selected Works,* p. 180.
7. "Tactics and Strategy of the Latin American Revolution" (1962), *Selected Works,* p. 85; and "Message," ibid., p. 180.
8. Guevara, *Guerrilla Warfare,* pp. 26–27, 46.
9. Ibid., p. 28.
10. Cf. Guevara, *Reminiscences of the Cuban Revolutionary War,* p. 59; and Carlos Franqui, *The Twelve.*
11. "Message," *Selected Works,* p. 180.
12. Claude Julien, Foreword to *Fidel Castro parle,* p. 12.
13. Marx, "Der Kommunismus des Rheinischen Beobachters," in *Marx and Engels on Religion,* p. 83 (translation modified).
14. "Budgetary System," *Selected Works,* p. 113; "Socialism and Man," ibid., pp. 162, 169.

Part II: Che's economic ideas
Introduction

Che's economic ideas, no less than his theory of guerrilla warfare, constitute an original contribution that enriches Marxist theory, a contribution based on the concrete praxis of the Cuban Revolution. This body of ideas is at once consistent with Che's principles of revolutionary humanism and adapted in a flexible way to the realities of Cuba's economic development. It was worked out during the great economic debate that took place in Cuba in the years 1963–1964, a debate which related not only to the island's immediate economic problems but also to the key concepts of Marxist theory and to the profound meaning of socialism itself, a debate which has its place among the developing conflicts between various tendencies within the international communist movement.

In Cuba this debate assumed a character that was practically without precedent in a socialist country since the death of Lenin: it proceeded in an atmosphere of dignity and mutual respect, openly and publicly, in the pages of the press. All the participants, who included ministers, leaders of the Cuban party, and European economists, were Marxist militants identifying themselves with the aims of the Cuban Revolution, and accepted each other as such, regardless of their divergent views. The debate did not conclude with a "disgracing of the vanquished": on the contrary, despite Guevara's departure from the scene, it was his views that prevailed.

The chief themes under discussion were: (1) problems of economic policy: budgetary system versus the financial autonomy of enterprises, moral versus material incentives;

(2) problems of political economy: the law of value and planning, the correspondence between productive forces and production relations, the commodity versus the non-commodity nature of the state-owned means of production; (3) general problems of Marxist theory: the role of consciousness in the building of socialism, etc.[1] I shall endeavor, in the pages that follow, to systematize Che's economic ideas around certain axes which give them structure, to juxtapose them with the other views that appeared during the debate, and to relate all this to certain "classical" themes of Marxism.

Note

1. Here is a list of the participants, their contributions, and the original place of publication of their articles, in chronological order. (For clarity, the titles of the articles have, here and in the text, been translated into English whether or not they appeared in English-language versions.—Trans.)

Ernesto Che Guevara, Minister of Industries. "Considerations Regarding Costs of Production as the Basis for Economic Analysis of Enterprises Under the Budgetary System," *Nuestra Industria*, no. 1 (June 1963).

Luis Alvarez Rom, Minister of Finance. "The Political and Economic Content of the State Budget," *Trimester: suplemento del Directorio Financiero*, no. 6 (May–June 1963).

Alberto Mora, Minister of Foreign Trade. "About the Question of the Operation of the Law of Value in the Cuban Economy of Today," *Comercio exterior* (June 1963).

Guevara. "On the Conception of Value: In Reply to Certain Statements" (reply to Mora), *Nuestra Industria*, no. 2 (October 1963).

Miguel Cossió. "Contribution to the Debate on the Law of Value," *Nuestra Industria*, no. 4 (December 1963).

Marcelo Fernández Font (Chairman of the National Bank). "Development and Functions of Socialist Banking in Cuba," *Cuba socialista*, no. 30 (February 1964).

Guevara. "On the Budgetary System of Finance," *Nuestra Industria,* no. 5 (February 1964).

Guevara. "Banking, Credit, and Socialism" (reply to Fernández Font), *Cuba socialista,* no. 31 (March 1964).

Charles Bettelheim (Marxist economist, Director of Studies at the Ecole Pratique des Hautes Etudes, Paris). "Forms and Methods of Socialist Planning and the Level of Development of the Productive Forces" (refutation of Guevara's views), *Cuba socialista,* no. 32 (April 1964).

Guevara. "The Significance of Socialist Planning" (reply to Bettelheim), *Cuba socialista,* no. 34 (June 1964).

Ernest Mandel (Marxist economist, editor of the Belgian weekly *La Gauche,* Trotskyist leader). "The Commodity Categories in the Transition Period" (reply to Bettelheim), *Nuestra Industria,* no. 7 (June 1964).

Juan Infante. "Characteristic Features of the Functioning of a Self-Financed Enterprise," *Cuba socialista,* no. 34 (June 1964).

Alvarez Rom. "On the Method of Analyzing Systems of Financing," *Cuba socialista,* no. 35 (July 1964).

Guevara. "A New Attitude to Labor" (speech to a workers' meeting on August 15, 1964), *Obra revolucionaria,* no. 21 (1964).

Alexis Codena. "Experiences in Supervision Under the Budgetary System," *Nuestra Industria,* no. 10 (December 1964).

Mario Rodríguez Escalona. "The General Conception of Finance in the History of the Budgetary System of Financing in the Transition Period," *Nuestra Industria,* no. 10 (December 1964).

Guevara. "Planning and Men" (verbatim record of conversations held at the Ministry of Industries during 1964), *Il Manifesto,* no. 7 (December 1969).

Fidel Castro. Speech on the sixth anniversary of the Committees for Defense of the Revolution (official adoption of Che's views), *Granma,* September 28, 1966.

See also two articles by Carlos Rafael Rodríguez, director of the National Institute of Agrarian Reform, defending financial self-management in the agricultural enterprises, but without taking a direct part in the discussion: "Four Years of Agrarian Reform," *Cuba socialista,* no. 21 (May 1963), and "The New Path of Cuban Agriculture," *Cuba socialista,* no. 27 (November 1963).

Here is a brief bibliography of works on this discussion:

de Santis, Sergio. "Debate sobre la gestión socialista en Cuba." In *Cuba: una revolución en marcha.* Paris: Ruedo Ibérico, 1967.

Dumont, René. *Cuba: Socialism and Development.* New York: Grove Press, 1970.

Gilly, Adolfo. *Inside the Cuban Revolution.* New York: Monthly Review Press, 1964.

Mandel, Ernest. "Le grand débat économique." In *Partisans,* no. 37 (1967).

Müller, W. "Einleitung." In Bettelheim, Castro, Guevara, Mandel, Mora, *Wertgesetz, Plannung und Bewusstsein: Die Plannungdebate in Cuba.* Frankfurt: Verlag Neue Kritik, 1969.

Tutino, Saverio. "Dibatito economico a Cuba." In *Rinascitá* (July 11, 1964).

1. Productive forces and production relations

One of the distinctive features of the economistic tendency that is characteristic of vulgar Marxism is its one-sided and mechanistic conception of the connection between productive forces and production relations, which it sees as a one-way cause-and-effect relationship. This conception offers as proof of its orthodoxy a quotation from Marx's *Poverty of Philosophy* (1847) taken out of context, a quotation that is endlessly repeated and treated as providing the quintessence of historical materialism: "The handmill gives you society with the feudal lord; the steam mill, society with the industrial capitalist."[1] Apart from the fact that this statement is wrong as regards the facts (according to the Marxist historian Charles Parain, Marx is mistaken, since it is the *water* mill that is typical of feudalism, and the *machine tool,* not the steam mill, that is characteristic of the beginnings of industrial capitalism[2]), it tends, if taken in isolation, toward a false methodological approach. A reading of the whole of *The Poverty of Philosophy,* and, above all, of *Capital,* shows clearly that for Marx production relations are not always and everywhere the reflection, or the effect, of productive forces; in periods of transition they can become displaced from each other, with the production relations sometimes acting as a brake on the productive forces and sometimes being in advance of them. As regards this latter possibility, which is what interests us in the present context, we can take as an example (given in *Capital*) manufacture and wage-earning work done at home—capitalist production relations which appear in the period of transition from the feudal mode of production to the capitalist mode, on the basis of the old, traditional productive forces (techniques, means of production, etc.).[3]

Among the Russian Marxists, the economistic tendency, most fully embodied in Menshevism, laid it down as irrefutable dogma that a socialist revolution was impossible in Russia: the low level of development of the productive forces would not permit any form of socialist production relations to be established. Lenin answered this view (after 1917) with two series of arguments:

1. The contradiction between productive forces and production relations has to be understood on the scale of the world capitalist system, a system in which, by virtue of its specific conjuncture in 1917, Russia is the weakest link.

2. Why not develop the productive forces in Russia by socialist methods, since the October Revolution has "offered us the opportunity to create the fundamental requisites of civilization in a different way from that of the West European countries"[4]?

Stalin's thinking represents, in this context as in some others, a half-return to Menshevik views. For Stalin there is an "economic law that the relations of production must necessarily conform with the character of the productive forces." He adds, moreover, that "the words 'full conformity' must not be understood in the absolute sense," because "the productive forces ... undeniably move in advance of the relations of production even under socialism." As for the October Revolution, why, the working class merely made use of the law of necessary conformity, adapting the production relations to the productive forces in Russia! In other words, Stalin accepts the premises of the Menshevik schema and tries to reconcile them with Bolshevism and with the reality of the October Revolution.[5]

How did the participants in the Cuban debate of 1963–1964 stand in relation to these "classical" points of view?

It was Charles Bettelheim, the French economist, who drew up the most thoroughgoing critique of Che's views. (In the pages that follow, Bettelheim will figure somewhat as the butt of my arguments. Let me therefore say at once, so as to avoid any misunderstanding, that I regard him as one of the greatest Marxist economists living and that in criticizing some of his views of that time—views which I think he has now largely abandoned—I do not in any way wish to throw doubt upon the scientific interest of his works or the revolutionary political alignment of their author. Besides, Che himself made a point of mentioning, in the course of a polemic against him, that "Comrade Bettelheim's article . . . is of real importance for us, since it comes from a highly learned Marxist and theoretician."[6]) Bettelheim appeals explicitly to Stalin's ideas and his "law of necessary conformity," and in accordance with this declares categorically that "it is the level of development of the productive forces that determines the nature of the production relations." Concretely, the necessary survival of commodity categories and the financial autonomy of enterprises in economies that are in transition to socialism "are bound up with a particular stage of the productive forces." (This would seem to imply that with the growth of the productive forces the commodity categories wither away; but that is denied by Bettelheim himself when he says that "the increasingly complex character of the Soviet economy and the other socialist economies" explains "why more attention has had to be given to these [commodity] categories."[7])

This conception was criticized by Che, and Bettelheim replied in an article in February 1966: "Che Guevara correctly criticizes—but mistakenly ascribes to me—a 'mechanistic' conception of the law of conformity between the level of development of the productive forces and the character of the production relations." Bettelheim thus recognized at that time that the transition period is "a period marked precisely by the circumstance that the new property relations and production relations are 'in advance' of the local level of development of the productive forces."[8]

This is plainly the opposite of what he stated in his article of January 1964, which Che rightly described as being mechanistic. Furthermore, a month later (in April 1966), Bettelheim went back to his former thesis by stating that "if we try to apply forms of organization and forms of circulation to the level of development attained by the productive forces, we shall achieve only a great deal of waste. . . ."[9]

As for Guevara, in his article disputing Bettelheim ("The Significance of Socialist Planning," June 1964), he refers precisely to the "weakest link" proposition and Lenin's polemic against the Mensheviks, whose relevance to an understanding of the Cuban Revolution he points out: in Cuba in 1959–1962, as in Russia in 1917–1918, a socialist revolution was accomplished despite the backwardness and underdevelopment of the productive forces. And what applies to the socialist revolution applies also to the socialist production relations it introduces: "To say that the 'consolidated enterprise' system [a socialist production relation challenged by Bettelheim] is an aberration is roughly equivalent to saying that the Cuban Revolution is an aberration. They are similar concepts and stem from the same analysis."[10]

In other words, one cannot deny the fact that the production relations in a society in transition to socialism are in advance of the productive forces without denying the very possibility of a socialist revolution in a backward country—semifeudal, semicolonial, underdeveloped, etc.

The (methodological) lesson to be drawn from history is, in Che's view, that a *dialectical* approach to the problem is needed, appreciating that the production relations are not always and everywhere "a faithful reflection of the development of the productive forces." In some transition periods the two levels do not coincide completely; in particular, "at a moment when a new society appears to smash the old one, and while the old society is breaking up; when the new one, whose relationships of production have yet to be established, is struggling to consolidate itself and destroy the old superstructure."[11] At these historically given moments there may be displacement, either backward or forward, of the production relations as compared with the productive forces. It is therefore not possible to condemn a priori, without a "concrete analysis of the concrete situation," such as Lenin made before launching the New Economic Policy, certain forms of production relations (such as the consolidated enterprise or centralized planning) by using the mere abstract and dogmatic argument that these forms "do not correspond to the level of the productive forces." Moreover, for the same reasons Che rejects the justification of the survival of the commodity categories and of financial self-management as forms "bound up with a particular stage of the productive forces"; that is, he rejects what he calls the "apologetic conclusions, tinged with pragmatism, for the so-called Economic Calculus [i.e., business accounting]," which Bettelheim draws from his method of analysis.

In both cases, this method seemed to him to be gravely vitiated by a narrow and mechanistic conception of the connection between production relations and productive forces.[12]

Notes

1. Marx, *The Poverty of Philosophy,* p. 109.
2. "Rapports de production et développement des forces productives: l'exemple du moulin à eau," *Pensée,* no. 119 (February 1965), pp. 55–56.
3. Marx, *Capital,* vol. I, pp. 362–63 ("the narrow technical basis on which manufacture rested . . .").

4. Lenin, "On Our Revolution" (in connection with Sukhanov's memoirs), *Works*, vol. 33, p. 478.
5. J. V. Stalin, *The Economic Problems of Socialism in the USSR*, pp. 9–10, 57, 55.
6. "Socialist Planning," *Venceremos*, p. 407.
7. Bettelheim, "Formes et méthodes de la planification socialiste en fonction du niveau de développement des forces productives," *La Transition*, pp. 138, 150, 147.
8. Bettelheim, "A propos de quelques concepts de l'économie de transition," ibid., pp. 166–67.
9. Bettelheim, "Planification et rapports de production," ibid., p. 190.
10. "Socialist Planning," *Venceremos*, pp. 402–4.
11. Ibid., p. 401.
12. Ibid., pp. 404, 409. Cf. also Mandel, "Las categorias mercantiles en el periodo de transición," *Nuestra Industria*, June 1964, p. 35: "In the period of transition from capitalism to socialism there is not *complete conformity* between mode of production, production relations, mode of exchange, and mode of distribution but, on the contrary, *a combination of contradictory elements.*"

2. The law of value and socialist planning

Marx, in *Capital,* defined socialism as a free community of producers controlling in a rational way, in accordance with a conscious plan, production and the process of social life. He therefore wrote, in his *Critique of the Gotha Programme,* that "within the cooperative society based on common ownership of the means of production, the producers do not exchange their products; just as little does the labour employed on the products appear here *as the value* of these products ..."[1] However, almost all the Marxist thinkers of the twentieth century (Lenin, Trotsky, Bukharin, Stalin, Otto Bauer, Luxemburg, Mao Tse-tung, etc.) acknowledged in various ways that on the morrow of the overthrow of capitalism it is not possible *immediately* to abolish all commodity relations and the entire monetary system of economy. Almost all the Marxist thinkers, that is, except Pannekoek and Bordiga, the two great "ultra-left" theoreticians of the 1920s, have rejected this conclusion and have seen, for example, the New Economic Policy in the USSR as signifying the restoration of capitalism.[2]

For Stalin the problem of the law of value in socialist society belonged within the general framework of a metaphysical theory of economic laws, according to which the laws of science, "whether they be laws of natural science or laws of political economy," are the reflection of objective processes which operate independent of man's will. These laws can be discovered, known, and exploited in the interest of society, but they cannot be changed or abolished "whether in the period of capitalism or in the period of socialism."[3] It would not be possible to overlook more

45

briskly everything that distinguishes a natural law from an economic law, and everything that separates capitalism, in which the "blind laws" of the market dominate the producers, from socialism, in which, according to Marx, man consciously controls the process of production.

In Stalin's view, the law of value in socialist society is precisely one of those objective laws that can be neither changed nor abolished, and consequently "our enterprises cannot and must not function without taking the law of value into account," a circumstance which, as he saw it, "is not a bad thing," since the law of value "is a good practical school which accelerates the development of our executive personnel and their growth into genuine leaders of socialist production at the present stage of development" by teaching them "to practice cost accounting and to make their enterprises pay."[4] (Stalin acknowledges, however, that in a socialist economy the means of production are not commodities, that the operation of the law of value is limited by the plan, and that it is destined to disappear in the second phase of communism.) In other words, Stalin seems to have regarded the survival of the law of value (and of commodity categories) under socialism not as a necessary evil, a legacy of capitalism which must be got rid of as soon as possible, but as an excellent training school for managing directors of enterprises!

In Cuba, the problem of the law of value was at the very heart of the debate, and it was no accident that the article by Major Alberto Mora, Minister of Foreign Trade, which "unleashed" the polemic, so to speak, was entitled "About the Question of the Operation of the Law of Value in the Cuban Economy of Today" (June 1963). Major Mora's main propositions, which implicitly rejected certain ideas that Che had already set forth orally and that he was trying to put into application as Minister of Industries, were these:

1. Value is a relation between limited available re-

sources and man's increasing wants.

2. In a socialist economy, the law of value does not disappear; it assumes concrete form through the plan: "It is precisely in the conscious decision of the planning authority that value most fully shows itself as the economic yardstick, the regulator of production." Therefore, in Mora's view, not only is there no contradiction between the plan and the law of value, it is only in planning that this law expresses itself "most fully"!

3. The law of value functions even inside the state-owned sector, which in Cuba does not at all constitute "one single large enterprise," as is thought by "some comrades" (you have guessed who he means).[5] Nevertheless, Mora, while referring to Stalin, Oskar Lange, and the "neo-marginalist" Soviet economists (Kantorovich, etc.), admits that there are also extra-economic criteria (of a political, military, etc., order) for determining investments in a planned economy.

The most profound and systematic critique of Che's theses, however, was Bettelheim's article, "Forms and Methods of Socialist Planning and the Level of Development of the Productive Forces" (January 1964). Bettelheim's methodological starting point is Stalin's theses on the law of value as an objective law of economies in transition. Indeed, he goes even further than Stalin, reproaching the latter for not having deduced all the consequences from this premise, in particular by denying the commodity character of exchanges between state socialist enterprises. According to Bettelheim, the role of the law of value in the commodity categories within the socialist sector is due to the too low level of development of the productive forces. Furthermore, at the present stage of development, society is not yet in a position fully to know the state of social wants, and, consequently, price "cannot reflect *only* the social cost of the different products but has *also* to express the ratio between the supply of and demand for these products."[6] Bettelheim's views were based on the present reality of the Soviet economy, the mode of operation of which he justified. In a subsequent article, disputing the Belgian economist Ernest Mandel (one of the leaders of the Trotskyist Fourth International) and Che, Bettelheim refused to bring this reality into confrontation with Marx's views, a procedure which would mean, it seemed to him, "according privileged status, to the detriment of practice, to the most abstract theoretical models." He explained this refusal with an argument in which positivism and pragmatism are harmoniously blended: since Marxism is a science and not a philosophy, "it is no longer a matter of measuring reality by an idea."[7]

Guevara's intervention in the discussion began with a polemical article against the views of Major Mora entitled "On the Conception of Value: In Reply to Certain Statements" (October 1963), in which he especially emphasized two problems: (1) value is not defined by Marx as a relation between needs and resources but as the amount of *abstract labor;* and (2) while it is true that the state sector in Cuba does not yet form "one single large enterprise," it is no less true that under the budgetary system as developed, the movement of a product from one workshop to another, or from one enterprise to another, is not an act of exchange, and that *this product does not constitute a commodity,* since the state owns the factories.

As for the problem of the general relationship between the law of value and the plan, Guevara expresses himself very cautiously, and we sense that his thinking on this subject was still in process of crystallization. He confines himself to noting that by employing administrative prices the plan inevitably "obscures" and "distorts" the working of the law of value.[8]

It was in two later articles that Che developed and deepened his ideas about planning, in open dispute with the *Textbook of Political Economy* of the Academy of Sciences of the USSR and with Bettelheim: "On the Budgetary System of Finance" (February 1964) and "The Significance of Socialist Planning" (June 1964). Che's central idea here is that planning is the "way of life in a socialist society—planning defines it and is the point at which man's consciousness achieves at last a synthesis and directs the economy toward its goal: the complete liberation of man within the framework of a communist society." In this sense, planning is essentially opposed to the law of value, a blind and invisible law which shapes the fate of the individual, a rigid and alienated order which eludes the will and the consciousness of men.[9] As we see, Guevara's conception of the plan is closely bound up with his ("philosophical") problematic of the conscious transition to communism and his notion of freedom as the abolishing of alienations. For Che, planning was not a mere technical device, but the necessary form whereby men dominate their environment, using the creative activity of the masses: "It is still necessary to accentuate his [man's] conscious, individual, and collective participation in all the mechanisms of direction and production," so as to break the chains of alienation.[10] In the last analysis, planning is the path that leads socialist society toward the realm of liberty.[11] Moreover, planning is now radically distinct from commercial business accounting in that it is not guided by purely quantitative criteria (profit, profitability), but by qualitative ones: use values, the satisfaction of man's basic needs.[12]

Che does not deny the survival, during an entire period, of the commodity categories and the law of value, but he stresses the fundamental contradiction between the planning principle and the law of value, a contradiction that has to be progressively resolved by abolishing the vestiges of commodity society. In other words, while recognizing that "for a certain time the capitalist elements will be retained and that this period cannot be ascertained beforehand," he explicitly opposes the prospect put forward by the Soviet *Textbook of Political Economy,* "to *develop* and use the law of value and monetary-commercial relations during the construction period of a communist society." For him it is not at all a question of "developing" commodity relations; on the contrary, the tendency should be, in his opinion, "to liquidate as vigorously as possible the old categories" (market, money, etc.). In this context Che criticizes the pragmatism of Bettelheim, who notes that these legal and commodity categories do exist in the socialist countries and then "concludes pragmatically that, if they exist, it is because they are necessary."

Concretely, this tendency means that while it is true, for example, that one can use elements of the law of value for comparative purposes (cost, profitability expressed in arithmetical money), prices will be fixed "with a manifest disdain for the law of value . . . always considering that a whole series of items that are basic necessities for human life should be offered at low prices."

Guevara clearly delimited the issue by stressing that he attributes to socialist planning *a power of conscious decision* much greater than Bettelheim recognized. Though both men accept the persistence of commodity categories, they differ not only in their evaluation of the role, the importance, and the significance of these survivals, but also and above all about the ways whereby they are to wither away. For Che, abolition of the economic vestiges of capitalism is not a distant and more or less "automatic" result of the development of the productive forces, but has to be undertaken at once, and progressively, through the conscious intervention of men, by way of socialist planning. It must be added that Guevara explicitly distinguishes between the centralized planning that he defends and the *bureaucratic planning* practiced in the USSR in Stalin's day; he even goes so far as to identify himself with the criticisms made by Lieberman—"We believe that his concern with the aberrations that the concept 'fulfillment of the plan' has suffered over the years is quite justified."[13]

The arguments developed by Ernest Mandel in "The Commodity Categories in the Transition Period" (June 1964) served to complete and reinforce Guevara's views. According to Mandel, exchanges in the socialist sector offer only the illusory appearance, the outward form, of a commodity relation, since the distribution of resources among enterprises is effected in accordance with a plan. Moreover, in a country like Cuba, to take the law of value—that is, profitability—as one's guide regarding investment would mean the end not only of planning but of economic development itself. It is obvious that in an underdeveloped country, agriculture is generally more "profitable" than industry, light industry is more "profitable" than heavy industry, and, especially, importing industrial goods from the world market is more "profitable" than making them in the country itself. "To allow investments to be guided by the law of value would mean retaining, in essentials, the unbalanced economic structure inherited from capitalism. Besides, generally speaking the greatest profitability from the national standpoint is *never* a sum of the greatest profitabilities of all the separate units." Like Che, Mandel does not deny the (partial) persistence of the commodity categories for a period, a persistence that he explains by the commodity character of the consumer goods sold to the public (until abundance makes it possible for them to be generally distributed). In his opinion, however, there takes place in societies in transition to socialism "a stubborn and long-drawn-out struggle between the principle of conscious planning and the blind working of the law of value. In this struggle, planning can and must consciously utilize the law of value in a partial way, in order the better to combat it on the overall scale."[14]

Notes

1. Marx, *Capital*, vol. I, pp. 50-51; "Critique of the Gotha Programme," *Selected Works*, vol. III, p. 17.
2. See on this Mandel, "Loi de la valeur, calcul économique et
   planification socialiste," *Les problèmes de la planification
   socialiste*, EDI (Paris), September 1968, pp. 113-14.
3. Stalin, *Economic Problems*, pp. 6, 7.
4. Ibid., pp. 23, 24.
5. Alberto Mora, "En torno a la cuestión del funcionamiento de la
   ley del valor en la economía cubana en los actuales mo-
   mentos," in *Comercio exterior*, no. 3 (June 1963), pp. 7, 10.
6. Bettelheim, "Formes et méthodes," *La Transition*, pp. 136,
   146, 149. It is interesting and significant that Bettelheim acknowledges (p. 147n) that "this analysis coincides to some
   extent with that made by O. Sik in his book *Economics, Interests, Politics* (in Czech)."
7. Bettelheim, "A propos de quelques concepts," ibid., pp. 164,
   172.
8. "On Value" (1963), *Venceremos*, pp. 280-85.
9. "Budgetary System," *Selected Works*, p. 128; and "Socialism
   and Man," ibid., pp. 157-58.
10. "Socialism and Man," ibid., p. 162. See also "Our Industrial
    Tasks," in *Cuba socialista*, no. 7 (March 1962): "We must
    create socialist consciousness by mobilizing the working
    people in connection with all the practical tasks of building
    socialism; for participation in the management of factories and
    enterprises, in the centers for technical education, and in the
    planning of the economy. In short, the people must participate
    consciously at every phase of industrial development."
11. Guevara wrote in his February 1964 article, more or less openly
    referring to the USSR: "We believe that in a certain way the
    possibilities of development offered by the new production
    relationship for promoting the evolution of man in the direc-
    tion of 'the kingdom of freedom' are being wasted." (*Selected
    Works*, p. 122.)
12. Ibid., p. 136.
13. Ibid., pp. 126-27, 129, 122 (translation modified); and "Social-
    ist Planning," *Venceremos*, pp. 407, 409.

14. Mandel, "Las categorias mercantiles," pp. 23, 27. Cf. also the summing-up article by Mandel in *Partisans*, no. 37 (1967), p. 30: "These who question whether the 'law of value' continues to govern production, directly or indirectly, in the epoch of transition from capitalism to socialism, do not deny that the commodity categories inevitably continue to exist in this epoch ... However, they understand the fundamental contradiction between the market and the plan, and so give great importance to the establishment of administrative prices in a number of spheres, either so as to ensure the priority development of certain social services or so as to ensure certain essential requirements for national economic development."

3. The budgetary system of finance

The theoretical discussion about conformity between production relations and productive forces and about the law of value was not academic. It had highly concrete implications in terms of Cuba's economic policy. The relation between the two problematics is plain: the finance budgetary system was criticized by the supporters of "business accounting" ("economic calculation") on the grounds that it was too far ahead of the level of the productive forces and in contradiction with the role of commodity categories in the socialist sector.

In the Cuba of 1963-1964, two models of management and organization of enterprises coexisted "peacefully":

1. In the National Institute of Agrarian Reform (INRA), directed by Carlos Rafael Rodríguez and administering the agricultural sector of the economy, decentralization, self-financing, "business accounting" of the profitability of enterprises, and exchange of products as commodities prevailed.

2. In the Ministry of Industries, directed by Che, the system of "consolidated enterprises," one for each branch of industry, was in operation, with a centralized budgetary system of finance. The governing principle was the realization of the plan, and movement of products from one enterprise to another did not take the form of a commercial transaction.

Carlos Rafael Rodríguez did not take part in the economic discussions directly. He restricted himself to upholding, in an October 1963 article in the journal *Cuba socialista*, the advantages of the "business accounting" system used by the INRA, while denouncing "bureaucratic centralization" as "baneful" for industry and "fatal" for agriculture. It therefore fell to Charles Bettelheim to provide a theoretical justification of the system of "business accounting," which he developed around two main themes:

1. The "consolidated enterprises" of the industrial branches of Cuba's economy did not possess *effective* capacity to dispose of resources, this being located only at the level of the actual economic subjects—the production units.

2. The insufficient development of the productive forces and the impossibility of completely knowing social wants make it necessary, in transitional societies, to maintain commodity categories and allow the production units a certain freedom of maneuver. This implies autonomy for these units as regards accounting, so that they are self-financing—in short, the "business accounting" system.[1] In a later article (April 1966) Bettelheim went so far as to write: "This economic situation finds juridical expression in the fact that each production unit 'owns' its means of production and its products." He adds that we are not here concerned "with what Roman law means by ownership, or with capitalist ownership," but with "a certain right of use and disposal."[2]

I have already analyzed Che's reply to Bettelheim's condemnation of the consolidated enterprises in the name of the "level of the productive forces." In addition, Che stresses that one of the starting points of the budgetary system of finance is the technical level of centralized management already attained by the imperialist monopolies in Cuba. Thus, the Consolidated Petroleum Enterprise, formed by the union of the three expropriated imperialist refineries (Esso, Texaco, Shell), retains and develops the economic centralization already achieved.[3]

According to Guevara, the Consolidated Petroleum Enterprises method was first suggested to him "by the practical experience of the first days of managing the industries" that were nationalized in Cuba. He also mentions as a source of inspiration the Soviet experience of the *kombinat;* and one might add the "negative example," so to speak, of Yugoslavia, where the system of calculating profitability was carried to extremes. In a piece he wrote in 1959, Che described with a very critical eye the working of the Yugoslav economy: "They practice something like competitive capitalism, with a socialist distribution of the profit of each enterprise; that is, taking each enterprise not as a group of workers but as a unit, this enterprise functions more or less as in a capitalist system, obeying laws of supply and demand and carrying on a violent struggle over prices and quality with enterprises of the same sort. They thus achieve what is called in economics *free competition* . . ."[4] Having said this, Che distinguishes, in the Yugoslav self-management system, between participation by the workers in the administration of the enterprises, which he regards as positive and which he tried to introduce in Cuba, and the return to competition of the capitalist type, which he rejects.[5]

The main features of the budgetary system of finance are the following:

1. The enterprise is not a production unit with a "juridical personality," but an agglomeration of factories (a "consolidated enterprise") having a similar technological basis and a common destination for their products.

2. Money functions only as an arithmetical element. The enterprises do not possess their own funds: their deposit and withdrawal bank accounts are kept separate; enterprises can withdraw funds in accordance with the plan, but their deposits pass directly into the hands of the state. These funds are consequently not commercial in character.

3. Business management is supervised directly by the central organs.

As regards the role and significance of banking in the budgetary system, Che makes brilliant use of Marx's analyses of the fetishism of interest on capital (in the third volume of *Capital*) in order to criticize the thesis of the financial autonomy of the National Bank in relation to the state. He does this in a polemic with Marcelo Fernández Font, his successor as head of the National Bank. He shows that this thesis implies that "the Bank finances itself out of its own resources," which would be absurd in a socialist economy, and that it falls into a fetishism that conceals the real production relations.[6]

To those who accused the system he advocates of having a tendency to bureaucratism, Che replied that, on the contrary, the more the operations involved in recording and supervising the work of the production units are centralized, the less bureaucracy there will be, the local administrative apparatus being reduced to the small nucleus concerned with managing each unit. He admitted, however, that the system was far from being completely realized in Cuba, and that it did show, in its current state, a number of weaknesses due to lack of maturity in organization, shortage of competent cadres, etc.[7]

Similar views are put forward by Mandel, who stresses, in opposition to Bettelheim, that (1) to expect to have a complete disposal of all the means of production, down to the last nail, is a somewhat mechanical and technocratic approach; and that (2) in an underdeveloped economy like that of Cuba, where there is a great shortage of technically trained middle cadres, it is even more necessary than elsewhere to reserve decisions of major importance to the central authorities.

Further, Mandel emphasizes the importance of associating as many workers as possible with the management of enterprises, so as to enable the creative and organizational capacity of the proletariat to be mobilized. The political implication of this is clear: as against the theoreticians of self-financing, who want to give the managers of enterprises the widest authority and autonomy, Mandel wishes to restrict this "stratum of managers" both from below, through local organizations of workers' management, and from above, through the central planning organs.[8]

Notes

1. Bettelheim, "Formes et méthodes," *La Transition,* pp. 141, 149, 150.
2. Bettelheim, "Planification et rapports de production," ibid., pp. 194, 195.
3. "Budgetary System," *Selected Works,* pp. 117, 119.
4. Cf. "Viaje del Comandante Guevara por los paises del Pacto de Bandung," *Sagitário* (Buenos Aires), June 1960. Cf. also "Il piano," p. 39: "The law of value operates in Yugoslavia; they close down factories on the grounds that they are not producing a profit; and there are delegations from Switzerland and Holland recruiting unemployed labor in Yugoslavia . . ."
5. Cf. "Interview by *Al-Tali-'ah"* (1965), *Selected Works,* p. 412.
6. Guevara, "La banca, el crédito y el socialismo," p. 30.
7. "Budgetary System," *Selected Works,* pp. 119–20, 132–33.
8. Mandel, "Las categorias mercantiles," pp. 12–14, 32–34.

4. Material and moral incentives

Among the themes taken up in the economic discussion in Cuba, the one that most struck the imagination of the public on a national and international scale was the problematic of "incentives." This was first and foremost a practical question of economic policy, directly linked with the controversy about systems of financial management. The supporters of "business accounting" and of the profitability of each enterprise taken separately were also advocates of the system of output bonuses, piece wages, and "material incentives" generally, and for the same reasons (adaptation to the necessary survival of commodity categories).

This theme also has, however, moral and political implications of major importance, which account for the intense interest that this aspect of the discussion aroused in Cuba and abroad. The decisive question is: how are we to transform men's behavior, how to create the new man? We know that Marx transcended the mechanical-materialist reply to this question ("Man is the product of circumstances: change the circumstances and you change the man as well") together with the idealist one ("Man must be changed first before society can be changed") in a dialectical *Aufhebung* that is brilliantly formulated in the third thesis on Feuerbach: *in revolutionary praxis the changing of man and the changing of circumstances coincide.*

What positions were taken on this question by the participants in the Cuban economic debate?

It seems to me that Bettelheim's thinking tends rather explicitly toward the pre-dialectical materialist pole. According to him, man's behavior is determined not by his consciousness (the ideas he has about his situation, etc.) but by the place he occupies in a given production process, a process that is itself basically determined by the level of development of the productive forces.[1] This leads, in the last analysis, to the conclusion that man's behavior will change only as a result of the development of the productive forces. A typical example of this underestimation of the relative autonomy and specific effectiveness of the ideological level (i.e., consciousness) is given by his analysis of the *kolkhoz* form of agricultural property, which he justifies as being the best adapted to the level of development of the productive forces in the USSR, and which, in his view, has nothing to do with any alleged "conservative mentality" of the peasants.[2] This amounts to saying that if China, say, has established, in the shape of the agricultural commune, a form that is much more advanced than the *kolkhoz*, this is not due to the political and ideological differences between the Chinese and Russian peasantries (and, in general, between the USSR and the People's Republic of China) but to the higher level of the productive forces in China!

Since man's behavior is determined by the productive forces, it is certainly illusory, dangerous, and harmful to seek to influence it by the widespread use of moral incentives. According to Bettelheim, "the respective places occupied by the different kinds of incentive are . . . not to be determined arbitrarily, in the name of some moral vision or some ideal of socialist society," but are necessarily related to the level of development of the productive forces, a level that at the present time requires retention of commodity categories and, consequently, priority for the system of material incentives.[3]

Guevara, on the contrary, defends a conception that is much more subtle and dialectical, and is synthesized in the now-famous little phrase from his article on "Socialism and Man in Cuba": "To construct communism simultaneously with the material base of our society, we must create a new man." This means, concretely, that this construction takes place around two "pillars" of equal importance, which must be accorded "preeminence": the formation of the new man and the development of technology.[4] He therefore rejects, as being guided by a "too rigidly mechanical outlook," those conceptions according to which material incentives will disappear by themselves, little by little, thanks to the increased availability of consumer goods to the people. These are conceptions preached by the supporters of financial self-management, who see in consumer goods the fundamental element in the formation of consciousness and do not perceive any contradiction between direct material incentives (to the individual) and the development of communist consciousness.

To this mechanistic (or, perhaps better, "vegetable") view of communist man as a fruit that ripens by itself when its season comes around, warmed by the caressing sun of material abundance, Che opposes a prospect like that given by Marx in his *Theses on Feuerbach:* it is through the revolutionary praxis of the masses, by constructing socialism *by socialist methods,* that both the economic structures and the behavior of man can be changed. The transformation of conditions and of man (of his consciousness, his character, his "morality") must be carried out simultaneously, the one in relation to the other, the one reinforcing the other, in a process of dialectical reciprocity.

Che thus rejects the economism that sees in the raising of the level of the productive forces the driving power of all social, political, and ideological transformations. He recognizes the specific autonomy of the different levels and instances of the social whole, and, consequently, the importance of politico-moral motivation and the need for what he calls *multiform action* to change the consciousness of the masses.

The material incentive—the mobilization of the workers by means of their direct, private, individual, material interest (in opposition to or in competition with each other) —is for Che a vestige of the habits of the former society, a society "systematically directed toward the isolating of the individual." As an ideological leftover from capitalism, it weighs heavily on the people's consciousness; it entails the risk of creating a disruptive atmosphere of egoism and striving to get rich, "which holds back the development of man as a social being." Guevara does not believe it possible "to overcome capitalism with its own fetishes"; a genuine socialist society cannot be built if the economic basis adopted is one that undermines, distorts, or counteracts the development of collectivist consciousness: "Pursuing the wild idea of trying to realize socialism with the aid of the worn-out weapons left by capitalism (the commodity as the basic economic cell, profit-making, individual material incentives, and so forth), one can arrive at a dead end . . . To construct communism, simultaneously with the material base of our society, we must create a new man."[5]

Another danger inherent in this system of rewards is its tendency to give rise to a privileged stratum of industrial techno-bureaucrats, who are the leading beneficiaries of "direct incentives." Analyzing the economic reforms underway in Poland, Czechoslovakia, and the German Democratic Republic, Che complains that the answer they give to the problem of productivity is "superficial": "They turn back to the theory of the market, they resort afresh to the law of value, they strengthen material incentives." But the worst thing, in his eyes, is that not only is the whole of the organization of labor centered upon material incentives, but "it is the managers who get more every time. It is enough to look at the latest plan put forward in the GDR, and note the importance ascribed to the work carried out by the manager—or, rather, to the payment to be made for this work."[6]

Having said this, Che admits the *objective necessity* of material incentives during the transition period: the new society is built by men of the old society. This kind of incentive must therefore still be used, but subject to the following conditions:

1. The material lever must not be the principal one; if it is wrongly given too wide an application, it "becomes an end in itself and then begins to impose its own force on the relationships among men."

2. While allowing this kind of incentive, one must fight against it and strive, through education, to hasten its disappearance.

3. The emphasis must be put on material incentives of a *social* character (for example, by favoring those centers of labor—maternity hospitals, workers' clubs, etc.—which have shown the most interest in building socialism, by giving them certain social advantages); or of an *educative* character (by regulating wages in accordance with the degree of skill attained and thus stimulating the workers to study and raise their cultural and technical level).[7]

Nevertheless, the historical tendency of the process of building socialism should be to bring about the progressive abolition of material incentives—with all the habits, scale of values, and ideology they imply—and their replacement by "moral incentives," that is, by the social and political consciousness of the masses. "The function of the vanguard party is to raise the opposite banner as high as possible—the banner of interest in non-material things, the banner of non-material incentives, the banner of men who sacrifice and hope for nothing but recognition by their comrades . . . Material incentives are something left over from the past. They are something that we must accept but whose hold on the minds of the people we must gradually break as the revolutionary process goes forward.

One type of incentive is definitely on the rise; the other must definitely be on the way to extinction. Material incentives will not play a part in the new society being created; they will die out as we advance. We must establish the conditions under which this type of motivation that is operative today will increasingly lose its importance and be replaced by non-material incentives such as the sense of duty and the new revolutionary way of thinking."[8]

To a certain extent one can say that the supporters of private material incentives were merely proposing a more or less mechanical transposition to Cuba of the Soviet (and East European) model, whereas Guevara gave expression to the special feature of the Cuban Revolution: the active and enthusiastic support rendered by the widest masses of the people to the carrying out of the revolutionary task. It seems that it was above all the experience of the extraordinary popular mobilization at the time of the "rocket bases crisis" of October 1962 that convinced Che of the superiority of moral incentives, not just politically but also economically. An analysis of labor during that October made by the directorate of the Ministry of Industries showed that despite the mobilization in the trenches of a third or even a half of the workers in certain industries, production plans were completely fulfilled, and in many cases overfulfilled, and a number of problems—low output, absenteeism, etc.—which had previously existed entirely disappeared.[9] This was, of course, an extreme situation, but like all such situations it served to *reveal* what was latently there by baring something very important and very profound in the economic and social behavior of the working masses. It was on the basis of real and concrete experiences such as this that Che put forward the bold hypothesis that "in a relatively short time, the development of consciousness does more for production development than material incentives."[10]

Clearly, this economic reason was not the only one that

led Che to prefer moral incentives. Whereas a system based on material incentives tends (as is shown by the Soviet experience) to "privatize" and depoliticize the lives of citizens, Che's economic method seeks to make permanent the "October spirit," the political mobilization and uninterrupted development of the revolution. If he believed that the instrument for mobilizing the masses must be "fundamentally ethical in character" ("without omitting to make correct use of material incentives, especially in social forms"), it was because this road is the only one that really leads to the communist future and the creation of the new man, the only one that develops and builds revolutionary consciousness, establishing the ideological hegemony of communist values.

We thus see the relation between Che's economic thinking and his revolutionary humanism. This does not mean that his economic theses arise from some sort of moralistic idealism: what we have here is a lucid and realistic appreciation of the dialectical relation between means and end in the historical process of transition to socialism. This dialectic is such that certain means *cannot* lead to the desired end. Saturating the whole of social life with psychological motives of enrichment and the real phenomena of the struggle to achieve it, racing for individual success, has dissolving effects on class consciousness and so creates dangerous obstacles on the road to socialism.[11]

In the last analysis, what was at stake in the Cuban economic debate, and in the discussion on incentives in particular, was the very meaning of socialism, the actual nature of the end to be attained. On this subject Che made a radical, striking, and passionate declaration in July 1963 which set the problem in its true terms: "Economic socialism without communist morality does not interest me. We are fighting against poverty, yes, but also against alienation. One of the fundamental aims of Marxism is to bring about the disappearance of material interest, the 'what's in it for me' factor, and profit from men's psychological motivation. Marx was concerned equally with economic facts and with their translation into men's minds. He called that 'a fact of consciousness.' If communism fails to pay attention to the facts of consciousness, it may be a method of distribution, but it is no longer a revolutionary morality."[12] It is in the light of his profound conception of socialism as a society that is *qualitatively* different from capitalist society, and not as a statized imitation of bourgeois consumer society, that Che's rejection of the Soviet model for the building of socialism has to be understood. This rejection he expressed very early on. René Dumont reports the following conversation in August 1960: "He was very critical of the industrial success of the Soviet Union, where, he said, everybody works and strives and tries to go beyond his quota, but only to earn more money. He did not think the Soviet Man was really a new sort of man, for he did not find him any different, really, from a Yankee. He refused to consciously participate in the creation in Cuba 'of a second American society, even if everything belongs to the State.' "[13]

Because his criticism of this model was a criticism *from the left,* it quickly became suspect to the "orthodox" as "Trotskyist heresy." On this subject the report he made in 1964 (to his colleagues in the Ministry of Industries) about the discussions he had had with Soviet students in Moscow is particularly illuminating. Che invited the students interested in having a discussion with him to the Cuban embassy, and delivered in their presence a regular onslaught on the system of financial autonomy of enterprises. He was amazed at the receptivity of his audience: "I had never before found an audience that was more attentive or more concerned, or that grasped my arguments more quickly." However, a section of the students—whose Bible, Che complained, was not *Capital* but the *Textbook of Political Economy* published by the Joint Academy of Sciences—

accused him of "Trotskyism." While politely rejecting this term as applicable to himself, Guevara made the following observation: "On this subject I think that either we possess the capacity to demolish a contrary opinion by means of arguments or we should allow it to be expressed . . . It is not possible to destroy an opinion by force, for doing that means blocking any free development of intelligence. From Trotsky's ideas, too, we can take a number of things, even if, in my opinion, he was mistaken in his fundamental . . ."[14] It is interesting to note that in 1961, in an interview with the American sociologist Maurice Zeitlin, Che explicitly condemned the destruction of the plates of Trotsky's *Permanent Revolution* (which the Cuban Trotskyists had wanted to print): "It was an error committed by a functionary of second rank . . . It should not have been done."[15] This remark is extremely important, both in its categorical assertion of the principle of democratic discussion within the Communist movement and rejection of bloody purges of the Stalin type, and in its violation of the sacrosanct taboo of anti-Trotskyism (without precedent on the part of a ruling Communist leader, since 1927 at the latest). It is known, moreover, that Trotsky's *History of the Russian Revolution* was one of the books that Che took with him to the mountains of Bolivia, where it was found by the army in a guerrilla hiding place in August 1967.[16]

Notes

1. Bettelheim, "Formes et méthodes," *La Transition*, p. 130.
2. Ibid., p. 139.
3. Ibid., pp. 151–52. In any case, for Bettelheim there is no place for moral ideas in Marxism, "which is a science." Cf. ibid., p. 170.

4. *Selected Works,* pp. 159, 163. Cf. Mandel, "Le grand débat économique," *Partisans,* no. 37 (June 1967): "Those who assert as an absolute assumption that the productive forces must be developed *before* socialist consciousness can come to flower are just as guilty of mechanistic thinking as those who suppose they can arouse this consciousness at the present time by means of purely subjective means (education, propaganda, agitation, etc.). There is constant interaction between the creation of the material infrastructure necessary for the flowering of the socialist consciousness and the development of this consciousness itself."

5. "Budgetary System," *Selected Works,* pp. 121, 127; "Socialism and Man," ibid., p. 159 (translation modified); Letter to José Medero Mestre, *Oeuvres III,* p. 317.

6. "Il piano," p. 39. This should be contrasted with Stalin's remarks on the social usefulness of the law of value, "which accelerates the development of our executive personnel." (*Economic Problems,* p. 24.)

7. "On Party Militancy," *Venceremos,* p. 243; "Budgetary System," *Selected Works,* pp. 121, 124, 125; "With the Workers of the CTC," *Oeuvres III,* p. 93. Cf. also Mandel, "Las categorias mercantiles," pp. 34–35.

8. "On Party Militancy," *Venceremos,* p. 243.

9. "Against Bureaucratism" (1963), *Venceremos,* p. 224.

10. "Budgetary System," *Selected Works,* p. 121.

11. Mandel, "Loi de la valeur," *Les problèmes,* p. 123. Cf. also the editorial in *New Left Review,* no. 46 (November-December 1967), p. 16: "Che was never more dialectically materialist than in his insistence on the primacy of moral incentives in the building of socialism."

12. Interview with Jean Daniel, *L'Express,* July 25, 1963, p. 9. Cf. also Che's speech of December 21, 1963, in *Pensamiento critico,* no. 41 (March 1968): "Communism is a phenomenon of consciousness and not merely of production; it is not possible to arrive at communism by mere mechanical accumula-

tion of the quantity of products placed at the people's disposal ... What Marx defines as communism, and what is generally aspired to as communism, cannot be attained unless man is conscious—that is, unless he has a new consciousness in relation to society."

13. René Dumont, *Cuba: Socialism and Development*, p. 52.

14. "Il piano," p. 37.

15. *Selected Works*, p. 391.

16. Cf. *The Complete Bolivian Diaries of Che Guevara*, p. 189; and H. Gambini, *El Che Guevara*, p. 490.

5. Voluntary labor and communism

The problem of the role, status, and significance of voluntary labor is obviously closely connected with the discussion about incentives. As unpaid activity voluntarily carried out by the most conscious workers, it is the most concrete (and most characteristic) result of politico-moral motivations.

In this sense it is important to Che not only from the economic standpoint—and it is known in Cuba how decisive this voluntary labor was for saving the sugar cane harvest—but also and above all as a factor that develops the workers' consciousness, as a practical, everyday school of political self-education, which prepares and hastens the transition to communist society.[1] Voluntary labor can fulfill this vital role because:

1. It constitutes a real link between manual and mental work, and a first step toward abolition of the traditional barrier separating them.

2. It is, or ought to be, labor that is "engaged in happily, to the accompaniment of revolutionary songs, amidst fraternal camaraderie and human relationships which are mutually invigorating and uplifting."[2] Che admits that this is something that has to be built, that is not immediately given, and he admits that he himself sometimes found his voluntary labor helping to harvest the sugar cane deadly boring.

3. It means a *conscious* participation by the workers in the building of socialism. It is thus non-alienated labor, free labor, to the extent that it is truly "voluntary," that is, the product of inner resolution and not of the external pres-

70

sures of the social milieu: "The milieu should help a man to feel this necessity inwardly, but if it is only the milieu, if it is only moral pressure that moves him, then even in voluntary labor the alienation of the personality will continue: that is, he will not be accomplishing something on his own, a new undertaking freely carried out."[3]

In this sense, voluntary labor already contains the germs of the communist labor of the future. In communist society, labor gains a new quality: it ceases to be an external necessity and becomes an inner need, a vital need, the expression of human creativity. Labor becomes art, play, creative pleasure, "a permanent and continually changing source of fresh emotions." Under communism man "begins to see himself portrayed in his own works and to understand its human magnitude, through the work carried out"—which supports the Marxist thesis according to which "man truly achieves his full human condition when he produces without being compelled by the physical necessity of selling himself as a commodity."[4]

Che's theses on voluntary labor and its significance for the development of the new man do not in the least refer to some "voluntaristic," "utopian" problematic alien to Marxism (as some of his "materialist" critics have alleged), but belong to an authentically Leninist tradition. In a pamphlet written in 1919, Lenin hailed the "Communist Saturdays" (*subbotniki*) that the workers were organizing on their own initiative: "It is the beginning of a revolution that is more difficult, more tangible, more radical, and more decisive than the overthrow of the bourgeoisie, for it is a victory over our own conservatism, indiscipline, petty-bourgeois egoism, a victory over the habits left as a heritage to the worker and peasant by accursed capitalism."[5]

Let me add, to conclude this chapter, that Che's economic theses have become to a very large extent the theses adopted by the Cuban government. In his speech of September 28, 1966, Fidel came out explicitly for priority to be given to moral incentives. A year later, in September 1967, he said to K. S. Karol: "I am against material incentives because I regard them as incompatible with socialism . . . What we want is to de-mystify money, not to rehabilitate it. We even propose to abolish it altogether . . . The law of value is meaningful in a capitalist society in which the economy is based on profit. It is meaningless in a socialist society. We have no reason, we who are in a period of transition to socialism, to conform to the economic laws of capitalism as if our aim were merely to run the old system more efficiently. We have discussed this point at length and have decided to free ourselves as quickly as we can from the servitudes of the market. Our planning must be based on 'labor value' and not on fallacious calculations of profitability or profit. We are already going to put an end to all financial accounting in exchanges between socialist enterprises."[6]

Notes

1. Cf. Guevara, "Una actitud nueva frente al trabajo" (August 15, 1964), *Obra revolucionaria*, pp. 401–6.
2. "On Being a Communist Youth," *Venceremos*, p. 212. Compare this passage, where Che is describing the young Communists helping the peasants to harvest coffee, with Fourier's naive but fruitful dream of the "attractive labor" of the community (which he contrasts with the "repugnant" labor of capitalism): "Behold at early dawn thirty industrial groups issue in state from the palace of the Phalanx, and spread themselves over the fields and the workshops, waving their banners with cries of triumph and impatience . . . singing hymns in chorus as they march . . . Each sees a confidant, a friend, in everyone around him . . ." (Fourier, *Théorie des quatres mouvements*, in *Morceaux choisis*, pp. 142, 150, 158.)
3. "Il piano," pp. 36–37.

4. "On Being a Communist Youth," *Venceremos*, pp. 214–15; "Socialism and Man," *Selected Works*, pp. 162, 163; *Obra revolucionaria*, pp. 397, 400.

5. Lenin, "A Great Beginning," *Works*, vol. 29, p. 411.

6. *Nouvel Observateur*, September 17, 1966, p. 13.

Part III: Revolutionary warfare

Introduction

Ernesto Che Guevara was not at all a moralistic dreamer, a utopian cut off from reality. His human and fraternal ideal of a genuine communist society (which I have been examining up to now) was accompanied by a lucid, concrete, and realistic analysis of the economic, social, political, and military situation in Latin America (and the other continents exploited by imperialism). His rigid and uncompromising adherence to the method of armed struggle follows precisely from this analysis: the new society can arise only on the ruins of the old world, the world of injustice and exploitation, oppression and lies, the world of the generals and bankers, latifundia owners and policemen, the CIA and United Fruit.

Che's sociology of revolution marks a radical innovation when compared to the conceptions prevalent between 1935 and 1959 among the Marxist Left in Latin America. (On the other hand, it links up, to a certain extent, with the initial period of Latin American Marxism, that of the "great ancestors": Julio Antonio Mella, Ponce, Mariátegui.) The history of the Latin American Communist parties in this period was one of continual setbacks, despite the devotion, courage, and spirit of sacrifice of several generations of militants. There can be no doubt that one of the reasons for this "permanent defeat" was the false understanding these parties had of the revolutionary process on the continent, an understanding based on the Menshevik-Stalinist theory of "revolution by stages."

With a few (local and temporary) variants, the following schema explicitly or implicitly underlay the strategy of

75

the Latin American Communist parties from 1935 to our time, and especially after 1955:

1. The Latin American countries are countries with underdeveloped, semifeudal economies dominated by imperialism; the principal contradiction is that between the nation and foreign capital (with its internal associates). This contradiction opposes the people, allied to the progressive national bourgeoisie—which is interested in independent national development, industrialization, and an extension of the internal market—to North American imperialism and its associates, the big landlords (the feudal latifundia owners).

2. It is therefore necessary to form a national-democratic front of the popular classes (workers and peasants), the nationalist petty bourgeoisie, and the progressive bourgeoisie, a front whose usual political expression is an electoral alliance between the Communist party and those bourgeois parties regarded as "patriotic."

3. The Latin American revolution is thus at the democratic (bourgeois) stage and must be accomplished by setting up a national-democratic government supported by the masses of the people. There is no a priori reason why this government should not come to power through elections, or by a coup d'état made by nationalist military men.

4. The principal tasks of this national-democratic revolution are agrarian reform, expropriation of the big foreign-owned trusts, legalization of the workers' parties, and an independent (neutralist) foreign policy.

5. The class struggle between the proletariat and the bourgeoisie is, at the present stage of the revolution, a secondary contradiction. It will become the principal contradiction only at the stage of socialist revolution, which lies in the more or less distant future.

Clearly, armed struggle and peasant guerrilla warfare had no place within a problematic such as this. They lay strictly outside the field of vision defined by this conception, a conception that in many ways resembles that advocated by the Mensheviks before the October Revolution. A typical example of this strategy is the "self-criticism" of the general secretary of the Brazilian Communist Party, Luis Carlos Prestes, drawn up in June 1959. A few months after the victory of the Cuban Revolution and on the eve of a decade of radicalization of the class struggle throughout the continent, and in Brazil in particular, this Dr. Pangloss of "official Marxism" wrote: "We have seen that as a result of the country's economic development, the contradiction that increasingly became more acute was that which opposed the Brazilian nation to American imperialism and its internal agents. This contradiction became the principal and dominant one, and determined the process of transformation in the alignment of social forces. Everyday conditions became more favorable for unifying broad forces against American imperialism and its internal agents, a front that can rally the proletariat, the peasantry, the urban petty bourgeoisie, the bourgeoisie, the latifundia owners who have contradictions with North American imperialism, and the capitalists linked with imperialist groups in a rivalry with the North American monopolies . . .

"We were not able to distinguish, in the world historical experience of the great October socialist revolution, between the essential features, valid for all countries, and those special and singular aspects which do not have to be repeated outside Russia. This was why we regarded the road of armed struggle as the only one possible for the Brazilian revolution to take, without perceiving that in the new conditions of the country and the world, a real possibility had appeared for a different road, that of peaceful development . . ."

1. Sociology of the revolution

The national bourgeoisie

Che's skepticism about a "revolutionary bourgeoisie" in Latin America originated in the experience he amassed during the many journeys he made all over the continent between 1951 and 1956. It seems that, in particular, he was not at all favorably impressed by what he saw in the "national revolutionary" Bolivia of 1953. According to his Argentinian ex-friend Ricardo Rojo, who knew him in La Paz, Che made the following caustic (and farsighted) commentary on that scene: "This Paz Estenssoro is just a reformist who sprinkles the Indians with DDT to rid them of fleas, but fails to deal with the essential problem, which is what causes the fleas . . . A revolution that does not go the whole hog is lost."[1]

Clearly, however, it was the Cuban experience that was to show him, with Cartesian and didactic clarity, the role played by the "native" bourgeoisie, who are seized with panic at the prospect of a revolution that undertakes radical agrarian reforms and the expropriation of the imperialist monopolies (in other words, the classical tasks of a democratic-national revolution), and who end by going over more or less rapidly to the camp of counter-revolution.

We thus find in Che's writings a lucid and disenchanted grasp of the status and role of this Latin American national bourgeoisie, whose political and social alliance with the big landowners he stresses—an alliance that constitutes the dominant oligarchy in most of the countries of the continent—together with its close economic, political, ideological, and (last but not least) military ties with North American imperialism.[2]

This does not mean that there can be no secondary contradictions between this local bourgeoisie and the big North American trusts. In the last analysis, however, the local bourgeoisie is more afraid of a popular revolution than of the despotic oppression of the foreign monopolies that colonize the economy. This is why "the big bourgeoisie has not hesitated to ally itself with imperialism and the landowners to fight against the people and close the road to revolution."[3] This analysis of the conduct of the Latin American bourgeoisie bears a remarkable resemblance to Marx's 1844 analysis of the German bourgeoisie —already conservative when they should have been revolutionary, timid when they should have been bold, and more afraid of the people than of the feudal monarchy they ought to have been fighting—an analysis that was brilliantly confirmed by the events of the German revolution of 1848.[4]

Guevara realized perfectly clearly that a Latin American "1789" was no longer possible: in the era of socialist revolution and the worldwide decline of imperialism, those bourgeoisies that had come late upon the scene of history could not but form a basically conservative force. This was especially plain in Latin America after the Cuban Revolution, which polarized the field of the class struggle: "The Cuban Revolution sounded the bell which gave the alarm ... The majority of the national bourgeoisie have united with North American imperialism; thus their fate shall be the same as that of the latter ... The polarization of antagonistic forces among class adversaries is up till now more rapid than the development of the contradiction among exploiters over the splitting of the spoils. There are two camps: the alternative becomes clearer for each individual and for each specific stratum of the population."[5]

Che was therefore convinced that, in contrast to the strategy advocated by the Communist parties, the popular forces had no interest in collaborating with those "timid and treacherous" bourgeoisies which destroy the forces they have needed in order to come to power. Further, he was increasingly inclined to give this diagnosis an interpretation that was not merely continental but was international when he noted what he ironically called the "South Americanization" of the semicolonial countries of Africa and Asia, i.e., the growing development of a parasitic bourgeoisie which accumulates huge profits in the shade of imperialist capital.[6]

On this subject, it is highly probable that Che knew and adopted as his own Frantz Fanon's violent indictment of the corruption of the new bureaucratic bourgeoisie of Africa, made in *The Wretched of the Earth,* a book that was published in Cuba on Che's express demand. There are, besides, a number of other themes where a remarkable affinity is observable between the ideas of Fanon and those of Guevara: the revolutionary role of the peasantry, the importance of violent action by the oppressed, the anti-imperialist unity of the Third World, the search for a new model of socialism, etc. Che took great interest in Fanon's work and had a long talk about it with his widow, Josie Fanon, in Algiers. It is even possible that his reading of Fanon may have been one of the factors that inspired his project for participating in the armed struggle in Africa in 1965–1966.

The socialist character of the revolution

If there is no revolutionary bourgeoisie, it is hard to have a bourgeois revolution: the definition of the character of the Latin American revolution was, for Che, closely bound up with his analysis of the role of the bourgeoisie. Only a socialist revolution based on an alliance of the workers and peasants can accomplish the democratic tasks of the Latin American revolution: agrarian reform, national liberation, escape from underdevelopment. But it will realize these aims not by the bourgeois path but by its own methods, socialist methods, along with the socialist tasks properly so called: Petrograd 1917–1919, Cuba 1959–1961 . . .

It seems that even when they were in the Sierra Maestra, Che and some of the other guerrilla leaders had an intuition (as yet vague and imprecise) of the socialist development their revolution would undergo: "The best among us felt deeply the need for an agrarian reform and an overturning of the social system . . ."[7] The radicalizing of the revolution after the seizure of power in 1959 took place in accordance with a rule that Che knew very thoroughly: "A revolution which does not constantly expand is a revolution which regresses."[8] As early as April 1959, in an interview with a Chinese journalist, Che spoke of the "uninterrupted development of the revolution" and of the need to abolish the existing "social system" and its "economic foundations."[9] This radicalization was carried through first and foremost by the agrarian reform itself, which, according to Che, differed from the three other agrarian reforms the continent had known (Mexico, Guatemala, Bolivia) by the unbreakable determination of those concerned to implement it to the very end, without any kind of concession; and, subsequently, by other revolutionary laws—urban reform, expropriation of the foreign monopolies, expropriation of the Cuban big bourgeoisie—laws which form a "logical chain that carries us forward step by step, in a progressive and necessary order of concern for the problems of the Cuban people."[10] This *logic* (which was at once economic, social, and political) is precisely that of the "permanent revolution," which leads from democratic tasks to socialist ones, from the struggle against imperialism and the latifundia owners to the struggle against their bourgeois allies, from the fall of Batista on January 1, 1959, to the proclamation of the socialist revolution on May 1, 1961.

This "growing across" of the Cuban Revolution from a radical-democratic revolution to a socialist one presents methodological problems that cannot be solved with the mechanistic and Menshevik-type conception held by the traditional left parties in Latin America, for whom underdevelopment—the semifeudal and semicolonial character of the economy—limited the revolution to the "national-democratic stage."

In Che's view, nothing could be more absurd than "to declare, like the theoreticians of the Second International, that Cuba had violated all the laws of the dialectic, of historical materialism, of Marxism." Against such a neo-Kautskian view (or, rather, howler), Che appealed explicitly to Lenin, whose famous dispute with the Menshevik historian Sukhanov he quoted in order to present the problem in its correct terms: *Cuba was one of the weakest links in the world system of capitalism.* This was why the revolutionary forces in Cuba were able to push on without a halt and "decree the socialist character of the revolution." The revolutionary vanguard, influenced by Marxism-Leninism, was able to "force the march of events . . . within the limits of what was objectively possible."[11]

Could what was true of Cuba also become true for the continent as a whole? In other words, was socialist revolution on the agenda for the whole of Latin America? From 1961 on, Che's thinking moved toward this conclusion, and in his "message to the Argentinians" in May 1962 he spoke explicitly of the socialist revolution as the only real solution for Argentina and for the whole continent.[12] In 1963, in "Guerrilla Warfare: A Method," he shows the link between the growing social polarization in Latin America and the character of the revolution that was dawning: the increasingly antagonistic contradiction between exploiters and exploited will mean that "when the armed vanguard of the people achieves power, both the imperialists and the national exploiting class will be liquidated at one stroke. The first stage of the socialist revolution will have crystallized, and the people will be ready to heal their wounds and initiate the construction of socialism."[13]

Finally, in his "political testament," the letter to the Tricontinental, Che presents the question in terms that are absolutely clear, sharp, and radical, bursting relentlessly as he does so all the multicolored and empty bubbles blown by Latin American national reformism: "The real liberation of all peoples . . . will, in our America, almost certainly have the characteristic of becoming a socialist revolution . . . the national bourgeoisies have lost all their capacity to oppose imperialism—if they ever had it—and they have become the last card in the pack. There are no other alternatives: either a socialist revolution or a make-believe revolution."[14]

By this stand, which is in line with Lenin's April theses and Trotsky's theory of permanent revolution,[15] Che synthesized in a bold, corrosive, and explosive formula both the lessons of the historical experience of the popular struggles of Latin America and a lucid forecast of the conditions for achieving the continent's future liberation.

To what extent is this formula also valid for the other continents of the Third World? Che did not express a definitive position on this matter, but in an interview in March 1965 in Algiers he declared explicitly: "Socialism or neocolonialism, that is the stake for all of Africa in the encounter now taking place in the Congo."[16] It is known, moreover, that in 1965 or 1966 Che took part in the fighting in the Congo, alongside the guerrilla fighters commanded by Gaston Soumialot.

Notes

1. In Gambini, *El Che Guevara*, pp. 79–80. According to Rojo, "Peron and Paz Estenssoro were for Che examples of a bourgeoisie that, through lack of self-confidence no less than through narrow-mindedness and absence of historical sense, got stuck half-way . . ." (ibid., p. 80). It should be added that in his appeal to the miners of Bolivia in 1967 Che mentions the way the Bolivian revolution of 1952 had become bogged down as proof that "where social revolutions are concerned there is no room for half-solutions."

2. "Guerrilla Warfare: A Method" (1963), *Selected Works*, pp. 91–92; "Cuba: Exceptional Case or Vanguard?" (1961), ibid., p. 70; "Tactics and Strategy," ibid., pp. 82–83; "Political Sovereignty and Economic Independence" (1960), ibid., pp. 222–23; "Message," ibid., pp. 174–75.

3. "Cuba: Exceptional Case," ibid., p. 65 (translation modified).

4. Cf. Marx, "Introduction to the Critique of Hegel's *Philosophy of Right*," in *Deutsch-französische Jahrbücher* (1844).

5. "Guerrilla Warfare," *Selected Works*, pp. 89–103. Cf. also "Tactics and Strategy," ibid., p. 79; and "Marxist-Leninist Party," ibid., pp. 104–5. A closely reasoned argument that supports Che's view is to be found in the works of the Marxist economist Andre Gunder Frank, *Capitalism and Underdevelopment in Latin America* and *Latin America: Underdevelopment or Revolution*.

6. "Tactics and Strategy," *Selected Works*, pp. 84–85; "Revolution and Underdevelopment," ibid., p. 355.

7. *Reminiscences*, p. 172.

8. "Guerrilla Warfare," *Selected Works*, p. 95.

9. *Selected Works*, p. 372 (translation modified).

10. *Guerrilla Warfare*, p. 115.

11. "Socialist Planning," *Selected Works*, pp. 402–4.

12. Guevara, "Mensaje a los Argentinos," *Cristianismo y Revolución* (Buenos Aires), October 1968, p. 22.

13. *Selected Works*, p. 101.

14. Ibid., pp. 178–79.

15. The similarity between Che's theses on the character of the revolution in Latin America and Trotsky's theory of the

growing-across of the democratic revolution into the socialist revolution in the colonial and semicolonial countries is undeniable. Nevertheless, it must be pointed out that Che's ideas regarding the respective roles to be played by the peasantry and the proletariat in the revolutionary war were, of course, far from being the same as Trotsky's.

16. "Interview with *Liberation*," *Che Guevara Speaks*, p. 119.

2. Guerrilla warfare

The inevitability of armed struggle

"He who wages war in a country when he can avoid it is a criminal, just as he who fails to promote war which cannot be avoided is a criminal." This saying of Martí's quoted by Che in his essay "Guerrilla Warfare: A Method" gives forcible expression to his deep and unshakable conviction that only the road of armed struggle can lead to the emancipation of the oppressed peoples of Latin America (and of the whole world).

Why? There is no question with Guevara of a romantic cult of arms, or of nostalgia for the times of the Sierra Maestra. The principle of the inevitability of armed struggle was for him derived precisely from the sociology of the revolution: because the revolution is socialist it can be victorious only through revolutionary war: "In America, the road to the liberation of the peoples, which will be the road of socialism, will be opened by armed struggle in nearly all countries."[1] If, indeed, the revolution in Latin America were only "national democratic," it would be able to count on the support of strata of the bourgeoisie, of sections of the machinery of state, and, above all, of part of the army, and could therefore be achieved by elections or by a military putsch. It was thus quite reasonable and coherent on the part of the parties of the traditional left, which aimed only at a bourgeois-democratic revolution, to envisage electoral alliances or military conspiracies as the most realistic strategy: given their view, it could seem nothing but crazy "adventurism" for the revolutionary vanguard to launch an armed struggle.

If, however, the character of the revolution is defined as socialist, then a quite different problematic is established, the Leninist problematic of the destruction of the military-bureaucratic apparatus of the bourgeois state. The question of "how to smash the repressive machinery of the oligarchical state" governs the whole of Che's politico-military doctrine: because his aim was a socialist revolution, he knew very well that the defeat and complete break-up of the army, its "dislocation," "dismemberment," "annihilation," and "moral destruction," are conditions that are necessary and indispensable for this revolution.[2]

The ironical skepticism shown by Che toward "peaceful roads" did not derive from dogma but from objective and realistic observation: even if a genuine (that is, socialist) popular movement were to win power by an electoral process—a very doubtful possibility in view of the falsified nature of this process—it would quickly be overthrown by a more or less bloody military coup d'état since the army is, as it always has been, the ultimate and decisive guarantor of the capitalist regime. Che thus arrived, by an analysis of the recent history of Latin America, at the same conclusion Marx and Lenin arrived at on the basis of the experience of the Paris Commune and the Russian Revolution: the revolution of the working people must smash the politico-military machine of the bourgeoisie. Che learned this principle not only by reading the Marxist classics but also from his bitter personal experience in Guatemala, where the revolution was betrayed in 1954 by its own army, which handed it over to the mercenaries of United Fruit; and from his triumphant experience in Cuba, where the revolution was victorious, completely smashing the reactionary army of Batista.[3]

The problem of the army is a key political problem in

Latin America, a continent where the military coup d'état is as rife as an endemic disease. Che defined the Latin American army unsparingly as a parasitic and privileged caste, "the visible head of the exploiters of every kind," and he showed himself free from any illusions about its "progressive" virtues. "Let us consider particularly the military coup ... What can the military contribute to democracy? What kind of loyalty can be asked of them if they are merely an instrument for domination by the reactionary classes and imperialist monopolies, and if, as a caste which owes its existence to the weapons it holds, they aspire only to maintain prerogatives?"[4] This does not mean, of course, that Che denied that the popular forces can absorb soldiers as individual fighters, when detached from their social milieu.

Consequently, the question of the army presented itself to Che quite bluntly in this way: "Accepting as truth the statement that the enemy will fight to stay in power, one must think in terms of the destruction of the oppressor army." Now, in order to be able to destroy that army, one must be in a position to hurl against it a people's army.[5] It should be added that, after the U.S. intervention in the Dominican Republic in 1965, protracted people's war appeared to him, with vivid clarity, as the only possible road, not only to smash the military machine of the local oligarchy, but also to stand up to the armed intervention of imperialism. It is in this context that we have to see what guerrilla warfare meant to Che—a tried, dynamic method of building the people's revolutionary army. I will endeavor in the following pages to bring out some of the political implications of Guevara's theory of guerrilla warfare, a theory that is profoundly "Clausewitzian," since it sees guerrilla warfare as the continuation of revolutionary policy by armed force.

Why guerrilla warfare?

From what sources did Che draw his theory of guerrilla warfare? In the first place, from Spanish sources, Spain being the pioneer of guerrilla warfare in modern times. In Mexico in 1955 he studied works on the military strategy of the Civil War in Spain, and he was one of the best pupils of Armando Bayo, the former officer of the Republican Army who trained the Cuban guerrilla fighters before they set off on their expedition. He discovered the "classical writings" of Mao Tse-tung only later, in the Sierra in 1958. After the victory he was to give close study to the experience of the Yugoslav partisans, the Algerian nationalists, and the revolutionary fighters of Vietnam. It remains true, though, that his principal source was his actual experience of the struggle in Cuba.

Why did Che see guerrilla warfare in the countryside as the surest and most realistic way to create the people's army? We find in his writings a series of arguments—economic, social, political, and military—to justify the special role he ascribes to guerrilla warfare in the overall process of revolutionary war.

1. At the economic level: In underdeveloped countries with an agricultural economy, where the bulk of the population lives in the rural areas, the revolution must above all be an agrarian revolution which develops in the countryside and the mountains, later coming down into the towns (where it becomes socialist).[6] This argument, taken in isolation, would be mechanistic: we know that Tsarist Russia, an agricultural country if ever there was one, undoubtedly experienced an urban proletarian revolution in October 1917.

2. At the social level: There is the terrible oppression and superexploitation of the peasantry, the wretched of the earth who have nothing to lose, whose social situation is explosive, and who consequently form "an enormous

potential force for revolution" (Declaration of Havana, 1961).

Analyzing the role played by the different strata of the peasantry, Che stresses that not only the agricultural proletariat, but also the poor small-scale peasants constitute the social basis of the guerrilla struggle in the countryside. Indeed, "the soldiers who formed our first guerrilla army of rural people came from that part of this social class which was most aggressive in demonstrating love for the possession of its own land and which expresses most perfectly the spirit catalogued as petty bourgeois."[7]

3. At the politico-military level: As Che saw it, urban insurrections, confined and held at bay within the limits of a city, usually end in the defeat of the revolutionaries and the massacre of the people. The revolutionary movement can then only start up again if, as in China, after defeat in the cities it falls back upon the countryside and wages guerrilla warfare. A people's army capable of beating the army of the oligarchy does not come into existence spontaneously: it has to be built up progressively in the course of a protracted war. A continuous and long drawn-out struggle like this can hardly be carried on elsewhere than in the countryside, which constitutes the weakest link of repression.[8]

4. At the level of military strategy: The countryside is the terrain most favorable to people's war: it offers most security to the armed vanguard, a bigger field of maneuver, lines of retreat, hiding places out of reach of the repressive forces, flexibility in action.

As for urban guerrilla warfare, Che, while recognizing its "very great" importance, seems to have underestimated the role it can play, looking on it as merely a by-product of rural guerrilla activity ("a suburban guerrilla band can never spring up of its own accord") and restricting it mainly to sabotage actions.[9] In the recent history of armed struggle in Latin America, urban guerrillas (the Tupamaros in Uruguay, various organizations in Brazil, Argentina, and Guatemala) have played a part that is politically much more significant than Che foresaw in his writings, in which he generalized too freely from the Cuban example.

Furthermore, the setbacks and difficulties experienced by the rural guerrillas in Peru (and in Bolivia) seem to suggest that he overestimated the security offered by the countryside, as compared with the town, for the armed revolutionary vanguard.

Guerrilla warfare as a political catalyst

Revolutionary war cannot develop and triumph in the absence of certain objective and subjective conditions. The objective conditions in Latin America are structural (the poverty of the masses, exploitation, underdevelopment, archaic social relations, etc.) or conjunctural (economic crises, dictatorial regimes, lack of legal opportunities). In *Guerrilla Warfare* Che presents the dictatorial political conjuncture as a condition *sine qua non* for the development of the armed struggle. "Where a government has come to power through some form of popular vote, fraudulent or not, and maintains at least an appearance of constitutional legality, the guerrilla outbreak cannot be promoted, since the possibilities of peaceful struggle have not yet been exhausted."[10] In his later writings, however, he tends to accord less importance to the presence or absence of legal appearances when an established oligarchical regime is involved.

As for the subjective conditions, there are essentially two of these, which complement each other and develop increasingly in the course of the struggle:

1. Awareness of the necessity for a revolutionary change of regime.

2. Awareness of the possibility of this change.

The oligarchy's power is based, among other things, pre-

cisely upon the absence of these conditions: on the ideological alienation of the masses and/or on their fear of the
armed force of the bourgeois state. The mistakenly op-
timistic hopes of a lightning victory entertained by the
men of the *Granma* expedition in December 1956 had
their source in a failure to appreciate the second subjective
condition: the Cuban people were aware of the necessity
for change, but they lacked conviction that change was
possible.[11]

This does not mean that revolutionary parties and
leaders have to wait with folded arms for these conditions
to mature and emerge. Against this sort of neo-Kautskian
passivity, characteristic of wide sections of the traditional
left in Latin America, against "the defeatist attitude of
revolutionaries or pseudo-revolutionaries who remain in-
active and take refuge in the pretext that against a professional army nothing can be done," not to mention those
"who sit down to wait until in some mechanical way all
the necessary objective and subjective conditions are given
without working to accelerate them," Che stresses these
two major lessons taught by the Cuban Revolution:
(1) the people's forces can win a war against the army;
and (2) one ought not to wait for all the conditions to be
present before starting the revolution—the insurrectionary
nucleus (the *foco*) can contribute to making them
appear.[12]

In other words, by its politico-military action, guerrilla
warfare tears away the mask from the ruling authority,
compelling it to reveal the nakedness of its violent dictatorship, and at the same time shows its vulnerability, its
weakness, together with the impunity and invincibility of
the guerrillas; it thus arouses the revolutionary consciousness and fighting enthusiasm of the masses and makes it
possible for the second subjective condition to appear and
strike root: confidence that victory over the oppressors is
possible.[13]

Nevertheless, Che was by no means a voluntarist, and he declared explicitly that the impulsion given by the guerrilla *foco* is not sufficient on its own to bring together all the conditions needed for the revolution. In order that the initial *foco* may be established and consolidated, certain economic, social, political, and ideological conditions must be already given, conditions that have to be determined by a concrete analysis of the concrete situation.[14] Che's position is thus precisely that of the Marxist dialectic, which transcends both mechanical materialism ("conditions determine the historical process") and abstract idealism (which asserts the omnipotence of the will): the praxis of the revolutionary vanguard is both the product of given conditions and the creator of new conditions.

By playing this part at the level of the consciousness of the masses, guerrilla warfare functions as a *catalyzing agent,* that little external element which, when introduced into a "favorable setting," provokes its crystallization and polarization. It thus plays a decisive political role not only in the area directly affected by its activities, but also at the level of the nation (or the continent!) as a whole. Commenting in his Bolivia diary on June 13, 1967, on the political convulsion brought about in that country as a result of the first victories of the guerrillas, Che noted: "Rarely is the possibility of the guerrillas becoming a catalyst seen so clearly."[15]

Thanks to its function as a catalyst, and to its politico-military activity, the guerrilla force can, step by step, win the support of the peasants and eventually become, in the eyes of the masses in town and country, the expression of their class struggle and a concrete political alternative to the established authority. In order to understand this process, we must examine closely the structure of the bonds that are formed between the guerrillas and the people, primarily in the countryside.

Guerrilla warfare and the people

Che's theory of guerrilla struggle has been condemned by the pseudo-orthodox as a Blanquist, Bakuninist, adventurist theory, built around the illusion that a small band of heroic and determined men can make a revolution, take power, and liberate a people, and seeking to substitute for mass struggles the miraculous exploits of a group of bold fellows of the swashbuckling "Three Musketeers" variety.

However, this was not Che's idea at all. In his "manual" of guerrilla warfare, he rejected the etymological meaning of the Spanish word *guerrilla* ("little war"), stressing that guerrilla warfare is not small-scale warfare, the war of a minority group against a mighty army, but, on the contrary, the war of the whole people against oppressive rule. In his article, "Guerrilla Warfare: A Method," he is even more explicit, criticizing "those who want to undertake guerrilla warfare . . . forgetting mass struggle, implying that guerrilla warfare and mass struggle are opposed to each other. We reject this implication, for guerrilla warfare is a people's war; to attempt to carry out this type of war without the population's support is the prelude to inevitable disaster. *The guerrilla is the combat vanguard of the people . . . supported by the peasant and worker masses of the region and of the whole territory in which it acts. Without these prerequisites, guerrilla warfare is not possible."* This is the lesson to be learned not only from the Cuban Revolution but from all people's wars, and in particular from the revolutionary war of the Vietnamese people, which provides the best example, in Che's view, of "organic" ties between the armed vanguard and the people, and in which "the guerrilla war is but an expression of mass struggle."[16]

This is also, of course, the lesson of the Chinese Revolution: in an interview in April 1959 with a journalist from the People's Republic of China, Che mentioned that during the guerrilla campaign in Cuba he had "carefully" studied the military writings of Mao Tse-tung and had "learned many things" from them—probably referring not merely to the strategic aspect of these writings, but also to their political dimension, the analysis of relations between the guerrillas and the peasant masses.[17]

First and foremost, it is the people (in the countryside this would be the peasants) who provide the best guerrilla fighters: they know the terrain, the inhabitants, and the way of life of the region, and are used to the hardships of life in the hills. More generally, the people are "the heart of the guerrilla struggle," present behind every operation; they constitute the invisible allies who watch the enemy, pass on information, ensure supplies, and grant the fighters effective support, cooperation, and generous protection.[18]

The peasant masses play this decisive role only insofar as the guerrilla struggle appears to them to be the expression of their class struggle. For this to happen it is therefore necessary that the armed action of the guerrilla fighter be an echo of the social protest of the people against their oppressors, and of the aspirations of the great mass of peasants who want to change the agrarian regime. In other words, the people must understand the political significance of the guerrilla struggle and make it their own.

This is why Che, without in the least neglecting the strictly military dimension of the struggle, insisted on the importance of the political work to be carried out by the vanguard, and defined revolutionary war as a "great politico-military operation" of which guerrilla struggle forms only "a part." The vanguard must promote, alongside armed actions, intensive mass work, explaining the motives and aims of the revolution, the victories of the guerrillas, and the reasons for each action. It must call for effective mass struggles by the workers and peasants: "Assaults and terrorism in indiscriminate form should not be employed. More preferable is effort directed at large concentrations of people in whom the revolutionary idea can be planted and nurtured, so that at a critical moment they can be mobilized and with the help of the armed forces contribute to a favorable balance on the side of the revolution. For this it is necessary also to make use of popular organizations of workers, professional people, and peasants, who work at sowing the seed of the revolution among their respective masses, explaining, providing revolutionary publications for reading, teaching the truth."[19]

We thus see how false is the picture that is given of Che as a romantic adventurer, a sort of Red d'Artagnan who saw guerrilla warfare as something like a duel between the Musketeers and the Cardinal's Guards. While giving strict and scrupulous attention to purely military and strategic aspects of the struggle, Guevara clearly understood the overall, politico-military nature of a people's war, and the capital importance of agitation, propaganda, and the organization of the masses for the revolutionary struggle.

Moreover, the political activity of the guerrilla force is not restricted to "classical" propaganda: it is also to carry out "propaganda by deed," both through its armed operations, which expose the vulnerability of the oppressors' army, and by applying, in the areas under its control, measures that are revolutionary in character: expropriation, occupation, and distribution of land to the peasants, the organization of cooperatives, the establishment of a court and an administration, the promulgation of revolutionary laws, etc. The guerrilla force thus gradually appears as an alternative authority in opposition to the established one, a new legality replacing the law of the state: a revolutionary authority and legality that serves the interests and social aspirations of the masses and neutralizes the repressive machinery of the dominant classes.

At the same time, the relationship between the peasant masses and the guerrilla fighters is not at all a one-sided, mechanical, one-way relationship, "from above to below."

In contact with the life, problems, and struggles of the peasants, "a revolution took place in our minds," notes Che, stressing the part played by this experience in forming the ideology of the guerrilla army. In the course of guerrilla warfare a process of dialectically reciprocal relations is established between the vanguard and the masses: "It happens then . . . that a genuine interaction is produced between these leaders, who with their acts teach the people the fundamental importance of the armed fight, and the people themselves who rise in rebellion and teach the leaders these practical necessities of which we speak. Thus, as a product of this interaction between the guerrilla fighter and his people, a progressive radicalization appears which further accentuates the revolutionary characteristics of the movement and gives it a national scope."[20] The close association between the guerrilla army and the peasants is not, indeed, something that is given from the outset; it is built up progressively in the politico-military praxis during which the guerrilla army becomes a people's army and the people become revolutionary, the two progressively merging into a more or less homogeneous bloc. From that moment onward the guerrilla movement becomes practically invincible, and is able progressively to defeat, demoralize, and overcome the army of the bourgeois state.

While it is true that the guerrilla nucleus cannot be a "mass movement" from the very start, is not a certain amount of political work among the masses in town and country needed in order to prepare the launching of the armed struggle? Is not the establishing of a politico-military network of support, shelter, and supply (both in the towns and among the peasants) a condition for survival even so far as the guerrilla nucleus is concerned? Must not the guerrilla struggle be linked up from the outset with the class struggles already going on in certain parts of the countryside? The answer to these questions—which were raised very sharply after the tragedy in Bolivia of 1967—and to many others cannot be found in the writings of Che alone; they will be given by the concrete experience of the new revolutionary vanguards waging the struggle in Latin America and elsewhere today.

Notes

1. Interview with CBS, December 13, 1964, in Gambini, *El Che Guevara*, p. 426.
2. "Cuba: Exceptional Case," *Selected Works*, pp. 63-64.
3. Ibid., p. 66; "Tactics and Strategy," ibid., pp. 78-79.
4. "Guerrilla Warfare," ibid., p. 95 (translation modified).
5. "Tactics and Strategy," ibid., pp. 85-86.
6. "Social Ideals of the Rebel Army" (1959), ibid., pp. 203-4.
7. "Cuba: Exceptional Case," ibid., pp. 60, 69. This should be related to the revealing statement made by the President of Colombia, Carlos Lleras Restrepo, in 1966: "I believe minifundia are far more dangerous politically than latifundia. These increasingly smaller properties cannot maintain a family, and the minifundia problem is constantly aggravated by the divisions imposed by inheritance laws and by the powerful demographic explosion . . . creating a class of 'proletarian proprietors' with even lower incomes than the miserable sugar cane cutters." (Quoted in Norman Gall, "The Legacy of Che Guevara," *Commentary*, December 1967, p. 43.) See also the statements of the leader of the rebel armed forces of Guatemala, César Montes, on the surprising success encountered by the guerrilla fighters among the impoverished small peasant proprietors.
8. *Reminiscences*, pp. 192-93; "Guerrilla Warfare," *Selected Works*, pp. 96-97.
9. *Guerrilla Warfare*, p. 37.
10. Ibid., p. 16.
11. "Cuba: Exceptional Case," *Selected Works*, pp. 63-64; "Marxist-Leninist Party," ibid., pp. 105-6; "Guerrilla Warfare," ibid., pp. 94, 102-3.

12. *Guerrilla Warfare*, p. 15.
13. "Guerrilla Warfare," *Selected Works*, p. 95; "Socialism and Man," ibid., p. 155; "Colonialism Is Doomed," ibid., pp. 337–38.
14. *Guerrilla Warfare*, p. 15.
15. *Complete Bolivian Diaries*, p. 168. See also the appeal of the ELN (National Liberation Army) to the miners of Bolivia, where Che writes that the guerrilla force "will grow stronger at the expense of the enemy army and will serve as the catalyzing agent for the revolutionary fervor of the masses until a revolutionary situation is created in which state power will crumble under a single effective blow, dealt at the right moment." (*Selected Works*, p. 186; translation modified.)
16. "Guerrilla Warfare," ibid., pp. 89–90; *Guerrilla Warfare*, pp. 17–19; Prologue to Giap, "People's War, People's Army," in *Che Guevara on Revolution*, Jay Mallin, ed., p. 106.
17. *Selected Works*, p. 368.
18. "What Is a Guerrilla Fighter?" (1959), *Oeuvres I*, p. 134; "Social Ideals of the Rebel Army," *Selected Works*, pp. 199–200; *Guerrilla Warfare*, pp. 45, 72, 84; *Reminiscences*, passim.
19. "Guerrilla Warfare," *Selected Works*, pp. 99–101; *Guerrilla Warfare*, pp. 22, 87. It is known that during his column's invasion of the province of Camagüey in the summer of 1958, Che made contact with the workers' and peasants' unions in that area, and even set up local associations of agricultural workers. Cf. Che's letter to Fidel of September 13, 1958, published in *Maquis* (Milan), no. 1 (1969), p. 53.
20. *Guerrilla Warfare*, p. 45.

3. The general strike

The guerrilla struggle cannot develop, become the fighting vanguard of the masses, and eventually destroy the repressive machinery of the state unless it is supported by the working class, unless it is backed up by a struggle in the towns, unless the proletarian masses are mobilized. This is the general experience of revolutionary war. Analyzing the history of the guerrilla struggle in Vietnam in his introduction to Giap's *People's War,* Che stressed that "mass struggle was also utilized in the cities at all moments as an indispensable weapon in the development of the conflict."[1] This urban mass movement, by its dynamic and uncompromising character, constituted in his eyes a precious example that is of fundamental importance for the freedom struggle in Latin America.

The role, significance, and influence of the workers' struggle grows in proportion as the revolutionary war develops and the alliance between workers and peasants is forged. In the initial period, when the guerrilla struggle begins, the urban mass movement (strikes, demonstrations, etc.) plays mainly a diversionary role, obliging the forces of repression to spread themselves out and preventing them from concentrating on the countryside. When the guerrilla army comes down into more densely populated and urbanized areas, it unites more closely with the workers' movement, which it is indeed dependent upon if it is to operate in this geographically unfavorable terrain. This was, in Cuba, the moment when Che's column invaded the province of Las Villas and captured the town of Santa Clara, relying on the trade unions, the Partido

Socialista Popular, the urban cadres of the 26th of July Movement, and the working people generally. Finally, once the army has been beaten by the guerrillas, an insurrectionary general strike is declared—a "most important" factor in the civil war,[2] crowning the revolutionary movement, delivering the final blow to the oligarchical state, crushing the last political maneuvers and palace revolutions by the army, and bringing about a politico-military fusion between the vanguard and the masses.

The Cuban Revolution saw three attempts at a general strike: the spontaneous strike of August 1957, which began in Santiago after the killing of Frank País; the strike that failed to come off on April 9, 1958; and the victorious general strike of January 1, 1959, which dealt the finishing blow to the regime. Guevara's writings are particularly concerned with the first two of these.

The murder of Frank País (the chief urban leader of the 26th of July Movement) on July 30, 1957, in Santiago sparked off a spontaneous strike which rapidly spread to the other towns of Oriente province (Guantánamo, Manzanillo, Bayamo, etc.), completely paralyzing them, and had echoes as far away as the provinces of Camagüey and Las Villas. The dictatorship crushed this movement, which had occurred without any preparation or revolutionary leadership, but the guerrilla leaders—Che in particular—realized that new forces were rising up against the regime and that it was absolutely essential to involve the workers in the fight for freedom.[3] The experience of the spontaneous strike of 1957, led, however, not to any "cult of spontaneity," but, on the contrary, to the development of underground activities and organizations in the working class centers, "to prepare a general strike which would aid the Rebel Army in gaining power."[4]

The unsuccessful general strike of April 9, 1958, was launched "by surprise" with an appeal broadcast over the radio (which had been occupied by the revolutionaries) at

11 A.M. The organizers wanted, for military and strategic reasons, to catch the government and its repressive forces off their guard. The workers, who were at work, did not hear the appeal, confused and contradictory rumors circulated, and in the end the strike did not take place. The few armed commandos who had risen in revolt were crushed, and a terrible repression descended upon the revolutionaries. Responsibility for this setback lay, according to Che, with the leaders of the 26th of July Movement in the towns (what was called the Llano, "the plain," in contrast to the Sierra), whose strategic conception was wrong in two ways:

1. In wishing to make the towns the center of the struggle, they underestimated the role of the guerrilla struggle, which they looked upon as merely a "stimulus" to a workers' insurrection.

2. In conceiving the insurrectionary general strike in a way that was narrow, sectarian (in relation to the other trends in the labor movement, especially the Partido Socialista Popular, the "old" Communist Party of Cuba), and putschist, they did not understand the significance and tactics of mass struggle.

Consequently, they called the strike of April 9, 1958, "without the slightest political preparation, without even the shadow of any mass action," using a clandestine surprise move to try to direct the movement from above without having any effective ties with the workers at the base. They sought to launch the strike by surprise, with revolver shots, without taking account of working-class unity, and, above all, without emphasizing "that the workers, in the exercise of their own revolutionary activity, should choose the appropriate time."[5]

These remarks by Che illustrate both the interest he took in the problem of the general strike and his thorough understanding of the *mass* character it must assume. (We may compare the writings of Lenin and Luxemburg on the

Russian strikes of 1905.) Both in relation to guerrilla warfare in the countryside and in relation to the insurrectionary strike, Che's position has nothing in common with the "Blanquism-Bakuninism-adventurism" that has been attributed to him by some of his self-styled "orthodox" critics.

Did Guevara ever envisage the possibility of an essentially working-class and urban revolution in the most highly industrialized countries of Latin America? He openly acknowledged that it was harder to form rural guerrilla groups in countries where there was high urban concentration, and he did not rule out a priori the possibility of a victory by "a popular rebellion with a guerrilla base inside the city."[6] In particular, he suggested that in Argentina—the most highly urbanized country of the continent—the radicalization of the mass movement may lead to the working class taking power.[7] Debray, too, recognized that in Argentina, "where Buenos Aires, Rosario and Córdoba already group more than half of the total population (twenty millions), the importance of the rural proletariat is minimal, in terms of their numbers, dispersion or weight in the economic life of the country. A rural *foco* can only have a subordinate role in relation to urban struggle in Buenos Aires, where the industrial proletariat is the prime force."[8]

But even if the revolution does not have the proletarian struggle in the towns as its principal strategic axis, and even if the social composition of the rebel army is mostly peasant, the revolutionary war must be guided by the ideology of the working class.[9] This was not the case in Cuba, until 1959, but in Vietnam a war of the peasant type was led, through the basic link of the activity and make-up of the army, by the ideology of the proletariat.[10] It appears, then, that Che regarded that aspect of the Cuban Revolution as an exception which is not likely to be repeated anywhere else.

In Vietnam, this ideology was concretely represented by a Marxist vanguard party which led the people's struggle for national and social liberation.[11] Is this a general characteristic of revolutionary wars? About 1963, it would appear, Che tended to answer this question in the affirmative. In his introduction to a symposium entitled *El partido marxista-leninista,* he wrote explicitly that a party of this type, "vanguard of the working class," must be the leader of the revolutionary struggle. He stressed in another article written in the same period ("Guerrilla Warfare: A Method") that being the vanguard party is not "a diploma given by a university," but "means being at the forefront of the working class in the struggle to win power."[12] Nevertheless, his subsequent writings do not deal with this problematic and offer no reply to the much-debated question of the relation between the party and the guerrilla movement. It seems that a number of Latin American revolutionary groups tend today toward a strategy based both on Guevara's conception of guerrilla warfare *and* on the Leninist theory of the party. The Bolivian tragedy of 1967 showed both the impossibility of putting one's trust in the reformist Communist parties and the need to build a vanguard organization, rooted in the towns and the countryside, capable of leading the struggle on all fronts.

The revolutionary war which develops through political struggle and armed struggle, through guerrilla warfare and mass strikes, must not only break the resistance of the "immediate enemy"—the bourgeois-oligarchic state—but must also be prepared to face up to armed intervention by the "main enemy," American imperialism, exploiter and oppressor of the peoples of the whole world: the revolution has to be conceived, in the last analysis, as a protracted war on a world scale.

Notes

1. Prologue to "People's War," in *Che Guevara on Revolution*, p. 106.

2. *Guerrilla Warfare*, p. 22.

3. "Social Ideals," *Selected Works*, p. 198; *Reminiscences*, p. 146; "A New Old Che Guevara Interview" (1959), *Selected Works*, p. 369.

4. "Social Ideals," *Selected Works*, p. 198. According to Che, to achieve a general strike "a series of complementary conditions is necessary which does not always exist and which very rarely comes to exist spontaneously. It is necessary to create these essential conditions, basically by explaining the purposes of the revolution and by demonstrating the forces of the people and their possibilities." (*Guerrilla Warfare*, p. 22.)

5. "Social Ideals," *Selected Works*, p. 198; *Reminiscences*, pp. 197, 208-9; "Notes for the Study," *Selected Works*, p. 53; *Pensamiento critico*, no. 31, pp. 58, 61.

6. "Cuba: Exceptional Case," *Selected Works*, p. 67. All the same, Che thought it would be better to keep the political leadership in the countryside, even in the urbanized countries, for security reasons.

7. "Mensaje a los Argentinos," p. 22.

8. Régis Debray, "Castroism: The Long March in Latin America," *Strategy for Revolution*, p. 44.

9. "Cuba: Exceptional Case," *Selected Works*, p. 68.

10. Prologue to "People's War," *Che Guevara on Revolution*, p. 105.

11. Ibid.

12. "Marxist-Leninist Party" and "Guerrilla Warfare," *Selected Works*, pp. 104, 92 (translation modified).

4. The world revolution

Internationalism

For Che, proletarian internationalism was not just an edifying theme for May Day speeches but was, as for the founders of the Communist International in 1919, a way of life, a supreme ideal, a secular faith, a categorical imperative, and a spiritual fatherland. The profound significance of Che's internationalism can be understood only in the light of his revolutionary humanism. Internationalism is the truest, purest, most universal, most militant, and most concrete expression of this humanism.[1] The genuine internationalist was, for Che, he who "feels anguish when a man is assassinated in any corner of the world, and feels elation when in some corner of the world a new banner of liberty is raised," he who feels "any aggression as one committed on us, any affront, any act that goes against the dignity of man, against his happiness anywhere in the world."[2]

Obviously, internationalism must not only be felt, but must also and above all be *practiced*, by real, active solidarity between peoples fighting against imperialism, and by economic and military aid from the socialist countries to the nations that have taken the path of liberation. Inspired by these principles, Che, in his celebrated and widely resounding "Algiers speech" of February 1965, called on the industrialized socialist countries not to put their trade with the underdeveloped countries on the basis of the relations of unequal exchange established by the law of value: "There can be socialism only if there is change in

man's consciousness that will provoke a new fraternal attitude toward humanity on the individual level in the society which builds or has built socialism and also on a
world level in relation to all the peoples who suffer imperialist oppression."[3]

For Che, however, proletarian internationalism was not
only a moral imperative for consistent communism, the
true political manifestation of humanist values, but was
also and above all a practical and real necessity in the
revolutionary struggle against the common imperialist foe.
The anger and anguish he voiced, in his "Message to the
Tricontinental," on the subject of the tragic isolation of
the Vietnamese people facing murderous aggression by the
biggest war machine in history, thus reflects not only the
revolt of a revolutionary humanist against the base and
unjust oppression from which a people is striving to free
itself, but above all the realism of a clear-headed anti-
imperialist fighter who saw in the isolation of the Vietnamese "this illogical fix in which humanity finds itself."[4]

A world strategy against imperialism

Guevara very quickly realized the continental character
of the struggle which had been begun by the Cuban Revolution. In his "Message to the Argentinians" on May 25,
1961 (anniversary of the 1810 anticolonial revolt in Argentina), Che referred to the historical precedent of the
nineteenth-century struggles waged on a continental scale
against Spanish rule, emphasizing the mutual aid given
each other by the rebel armies of the various Latin American countries.[5] He thus linked up with the "Bolívarist"
tradition in Latin America, while giving this tradition a
proletarian and socialist content.

It was probably, however, the rocket bases crisis of
October 1962, with the imminent threat of an American
invasion of Cuba, that brought the continental revolution

into the center of his thinking. In an essay written during
that period, "Tactics and Strategy of the Latin American
Revolution,"[6] Che affirmed his certainty that the United
States would intervene against Latin American revolutions
out of solidarity of interest and because the struggle in
Latin America is decisive. He concluded by speaking of the
need for a counterstroke to be organized on a continental
scale: "Given this overall panorama of Latin America, we
find it difficult to believe that victory can be achieved in
one isolated country. The union of repressive forces must
be countered with the unity of the popular forces. In every
country where oppression reaches the limits of tolerance,
the banner of rebellion must be raised, and this banner
will, of historical necessity, be continental in character.
The Andean Cordilleras are destined to be the Sierra
Maestra of America, as Fidel has said . . ."[7]

As for the Bolivian guerrilla struggle of 1967, we know
that Guevara conceived of it precisely as the first stage of a
continental revolution, the next ramifications of which
were to be in Peru and Argentina, and after that in Para-
guay and Brazil. At the same time, Che was fully aware
that the Latin American revolution was merely part of a
wider movement, of the immense movement of that
"humanity that has said 'Enough!' and is on the march"
(the last phrase of the Declaration of Havana, which became the watchword of the Tricontinental). His interest in
the world dimension of the war against imperialism developed with his travels in the countries of the Third World
(1959) and in the socialist countries of Europe and,
especially, Asia (China and North Korea) in 1960. In an
article of September 1959, published in the Mexican
review *Humanismo,* Che defined anti-imperialist brotherhood in Marxist terms, that is, in *class* terms: "Is it not
true that our brotherhood transcends distances, different
languages, and the absence of close cultural links, and
unites us in the struggle? Ought not a Japanese worker be

closer to an Argentine laborer, a Bolivian miner, a man working for United Fruit Company or a Cuban canecutter than to a Japanese samurai?"[8] But the factor that contributed most to forming his international strategic outlook was the revolutionary war of the Vietnamese people. Che belonged, in fact, to a generation—my own—for whom the war in Vietnam played the same polarizing role as the Spanish Civil War played for the previous one. It crystallized international consciousness on the world scale around a "revealing event." Already in 1963, after the first great upsurge of guerrilla warfare by the National Liberation Front, Che stressed that the Vietnamese were "front-line soldiers in the front trenches of the world proletariat against imperialism," and that their fighting front was extremely important for the entire future of Latin America.[9] And it was Vietnam that he had in mind when he declared in Algiers in 1965: "There are no frontiers in this struggle to the death. We cannot remain indifferent in the face of what occurs in any part of the world. A victory for any country against imperialism is our victory, just as any country's defeat is a defeat for all. The practice of proletarian internationalism is not only a duty for the peoples who struggle for a better future, it is also an inescapable necessity."[10] It was after 1965, however, with the development of the American "escalation" and the open and massive intervention of the imperialist army in Vietnam, that Guevara explicitly and precisely formulated his world revolutionary strategy, the first expression of which was his "Message to the Tricontinental" in 1967. In this glowing and incisive document Che developed the following themes:

1. Imperialism, the highest stage of capitalism, is a world system, and must be defeated in a vast and protracted confrontation on the world scale.

2. In order to fight against the common enemy of the human race, U.S. imperialism, the socialist countries and

their supporters must unite their efforts, regardless of differences. The form these differences are assuming at the moment constitutes a weakness, but the necessary unity will eventually be imposed by the pressure of the enemy's attacks.

3. In this gigantic conflict, the historical task of the peoples of the Third World is to knock out the supply bases of imperialism in the underdeveloped countries, which serve as its sources of profits and raw materials, and as markets for the products of the metropolitan countries, and which are today in absolute subjection to and dependence on imperialism.

4. We need now an overall strategy for a war against imperialism, capable of bringing effective help to the vanguard detachment of the world proletariat: Vietnam. That is to say, we must create two, three, several Vietnams, in order to compel imperialism to disperse its forces.

This was the first occasion in a very long time that a Communist leader of world stature had tried to outline an international revolutionary strategy that was not dependent on the interests of any state. In this sense, too, Che's ideas meant a return to the sources of Leninism, to the Comintern in the glorious years of 1919–1924, before it was gradually turned into a tool of the foreign policy of the USSR under Stalin. This appeal was, moreover, no abstract and platonic declaration. It was written in the depths of the Bolivian jungle, by a man who was trying to practice what he preached and who sacrificed his life to this aim: to come to the aid of the struggle of the Vietnamese people by opening a second front in Latin America. All this explains the resounding echo that the appeal obtained in every part of the world.

This message was addressed to the Organization for the Solidarity of the Peoples of Asia, Africa, and Latin America, and its central theme was the role played by the peoples of these three continents. This does not mean, however, that Che's conception was a hazy "Third World-ism," without any clear political content. Nothing could be more erroneous than the view of some superficial and equivocal interpreters of Che's ideas that, for him, "the real contradiction was not between capitalism and communism, but between developed and underdeveloped countries."[11] For Guevara, the world revolution against imperialism was conceived in class terms and his ultimate aim was, without the shadow of a doubt, to establish communism on the world scale. Furthermore, while he recognized that the fighting spirit of the workers of the imperialist countries had been weakened, he did not fall into the anti-European nihilism of Fanon, but, on the contrary, prophesied in his "Message to the Tricontinental" that in Europe the "contradictions will reach an explosive stage during the next few years" (May 1968!) and that the class struggle will eventually surge up in the very heart of the American imperialist metropolis.

Notes

1. The Cuban Revolution "is a revolution with humanistic characteristics. It feels solidarity with the oppressed peoples of the world ..." (Speech at Punta del Este, August 1961, *Selected Works*, p. 275.)
2. "On Being a Communist Youth," *Venceremos*, p. 217; "Marxist-Leninist Party," *Selected Works*, p. 111.
3. "Revolution and Underdevelopment," *Selected Works*, p. 351. Cf. also Che's "Message to the Tricontinental," in which, for the first time since the International Brigades of the Spanish Civil War, a call was made for the formation of international proletarian armies: "Let the flag under which we fight be the sacred cause of redeeming humanity, so that to die under the flag of Vietnam, of Venezuela, of Guatemala, of Laos, of Guinea, of Colombia, of Bolivia, of Brazil—to name only a few scenes of today's armed struggle—will be equally glorious and

desirable for an American, an Asian, an African, or even a European." (Ibid., p. 180.)

4. Ibid., p. 171.
5. "This was something more than altruism on the part of the revolutionary forces, it was a pressing necessity, an imperative of military strategy in order to secure a victory of continental proportions, because there could be no partial victories, no outcome other than the total triumph or the total defeat of the revolutionary ideas. That situation in Latin America is repeated today . . ." ("Mensaje a los Argentinos," p. 21.)
6. Not published in his lifetime, but published in Cuba in October 1968. In *Selected Works*, pp. 77–88.
7. Ibid., p. 86.
8. Ibid., p. 44 (translation modified).
9. "On Solidarity with Vietnam," *Venceremos*, pp. 289, 291.
10. *Selected Works*, pp. 350–51.
11. Andrew Sinclair, *Guevara*, p. 75.

Part IV: Guevarism today

No porque hayas caído
tu luz es menos alta.
(Not because you have fallen
is your light less high.)
—Nicolás Guillén
Che Comandante (October 15, 1967)

Guevara has often been compared, and not without justification, to the great romantic revolutionaries of the nineteenth century. It would nevertheless be a mistake to suppose that Che was a man from the past, a survival from another epoch, an anachronism in the computer age. On the contrary, he was the avenging prophet of future revolutions, the revolutions of the "wretched of the earth," the starved, oppressed, exploited, and humiliated peoples of the three continents dominated by imperialism. He was the prophet who wrote in letters of fire on the walls of the new Babylon: *Mene Mene Tekel Upharsin*—your days are numbered. And it is as a prophet of the future, of the new man, the communist society of the twenty-first century, built upon the ruins of decadent and "one-dimensional" capitalism, that he has become the hero of the rebellious and revolutionary youth who are rising up in the industrial metropolitan centers of Europe and North America.

Although based upon the experience of Cuba and Latin America, Che's thought is profoundly universal in character, and this is what explains the worldwide reverberation and influence achieved by his writings. For the dominated peoples of Asia, Africa, and Latin America, for the Ameri-

113

can blacks, for the "Third World" of Europe itself (Greece, Spain, Portugal), Che is the prophet armed of the revolutionary war against the oligarchy, the military dictators, and imperialism, the man whose writings on guerrilla warfare are enthusiastically studied and discussed (along with those of Mao, Giap, and Fanon) in schools and universities, in factories and villages, inspiring the activity of revolutionary militants from the *maquis* of Guatemala to the black ghettos of Detroit, from the forests of Guiné-Bissau to the outskirts of Rio de Janeiro, from the oilfields of the Arabian Gulf to the factories of Córdoba.

Guevarism means, in the Third World, rejection of rotten compromises, opportunist maneuvers, "peaceful coexistence"; rejection both of equivocal neutralism and subordination to the diplomacy of the rival powers of the socialist bloc. It means armed struggle without yielding an inch, people's war until the bourgeois army is defeated, permanent revolution until socialism is established. It means the historical initiative of the revolutionary vanguard which launches the guerrilla struggle and mobilizes the masses. It means the concrete international solidarity of brothers in arms in the common fight against the imperialist yoke.

Yet Che's influence has reached far beyond the limits of the Third World: his portrait has been carried by crowds of young people in huge demonstrations in front of the Pentagon, on the barricades in Paris in May 1968, in the colleges of London and the streets of Berlin. His slogan: "One, two, three Vietnams" has been chanted in Japanese in the thoroughfares of Tokyo and inscribed in Italian on banners carried in processions in Rome. How are we to explain this "Guevarism"—at first sight so surprising—of the new young vanguard in the advanced capitalist countries?

First, because, by his exemplary life and martyrdom, Che is seen as the purest symbol of the fight for the liberation of the Third World. Fallen in an effort to come to the aid of the Vietnamese people, at a moment when the war in Vietnam was acting as a catalyst of revolutionary consciousness in the metropolitan countries of capitalism, Che also became for these young people the shining symbol of internationalism, of their new internationalism, reborn from its ashes after the long night of the absolute dominance of chauvinism. Jeannette Habel, leader of Jeunesse Communiste Révolutionnaire, a French Castro-Trotskyist organization suppressed in June 1968, said at the Congress of Solidarity with Vietnam held in Berlin in February 1968: "The youth of Western Europe must take inspiration from the example of Che, the revolutionary who knew no frontiers. We must defend Che like a flag . . ., defend his conception of a new man, tempered in the antiimperialist struggle, his conception of the revolutionary man who is concerned with the fate of all the exploited, who fights without expecting any material reward for his efforts, opposing revolutionary violence to reactionary violence."[1]

Furthermore, Che's thoughts and deeds represent for these young people both an uncompromising, absolute, and radical rejection of the "system," and the revolutionary initiative of the vanguard to transform it. In one of his most brilliant writings ("The Contradictions of Late Capitalism: The Anti-Authoritarian Students and Their Relations with the Third World"), Rudi Dutschke shows how the methodological principles of Che's guerrilla *foco* have influenced the actions of the German SDS: "For the first time we have tried to master Che's theory of the guerrilla *foco* in our own political praxis. The problem presented itself in these terms: how and under what conditions can the subjective factor be introduced as an objective factor in the historical process? Guevara's answer, for Latin America, was that the revolutionaries do not always have to wait for the objective conditions for revolution to appear but can create these conditions by means of a subjective activity, through the guerrilla *foco,* the armed vanguard of the people. In the last analysis, this problem was and is still there, lying behind all our activity. In this activity, ought we to assume the permanent ineffectiveness of our political work, or have we reached a moment in history when the objective and creative activity of individuals cooperating politically determines reality and the possibility of transforming reality?"[2] These principles have undoubtedly also inspired other organizations of the new vanguard, helping them to transcend immobility, bureaucratic conservatism, and passive adaptation to the bourgeois "system," the senile diseases of the old reformist left.

Finally, the third aspect of Che's thinking which has fascinated the revolutionary youth of the countries of advanced capitalism is the new model of communism it offers. To the bourgeois philistine, Che was a utopian-romantic anarchist whose ideal of the future was nothing but "the childish vision of Elysian Fields without bureaucrats or soldiers, that eternal nostalgia for a 'saved' world."[3] The "New Left" of Europe and America, however, which rejects bourgeois and bureaucratic authoritarianism and the values of the consumer society, recognizes itself in the ideas of Che, for whom communist society must be a new humanity and not a statized version of American society. Whereas for Khrushchev (and for a large number of the traditional Communist parties) communism will become "attractive" in the West when the Soviet Union catches up with the United States in production and levels of consumption, for Che and for the Red youth of the industrialized countries communism must be much more than a new method of distributing goods: it must be a contrasting model of civilization, a new social, cultural, and moral world. It is thus not a question of competing with capitalism and "privatistic" bourgeois society at their own game, but of fundamentally altering the rules of the game. This is why the poor countries in transition to socialism, seeking by different roads to create a new society and a new man (Cuba, China, Vietnam), exercise a much greater power of attraction upon the young generation than do the relatively rich and comfortable countries (USSR, GDR) who are trying, by taking the road of "market socialism," to emulate North American plenty.

The influence of this theme of Che's thinking was particularly marked, where the vanguard movements in France were concerned, before and during the events of May 1968. As early as 1965 the Lettres (Humanities) section of the Union des Etudiants Communistes—which was to break away soon afterward and become the Jeunesse Communiste Révolutionnaire, one of the principal "incendiaries" of May 1968—published *Socialism and Man in Cuba* for the first time in France. It included a very significant introduction which contrasted the "goulash communism" of Khrushchev with the communism of Guevara, conceived not as a planned "super-consumer society," but as a radically different society whose moving forces, work, and leisure activities would no longer be like those of today. Che's conception of communism was combined, in May 1968, with Marcuse's critique of capitalist civilization, with certain aspects of the Chinese Cultural Revolution, and with Trotsky's criticism of bureaucracy. The fusion of these ingredients proved to be extremely explosive.

"Now is the time of the furnaces, and only light should be seen," wrote Che, quoting Martí, in the "Message to the Tricontinental." The Bolivian furnace of Nancahuazu has been extinguished for the moment, but its light, the thought of Che Guevara, continues to shine, kindling new furnaces everywhere in the world, casting new sparks in all directions, guiding the peoples like a torch in the darkness. Nothing will ever succeed in extinguishing that light.

Notes

1. In *Che Guevara und die Revolution,* H. R. Sonntag, ed., p. 106.
2. In *Pensamiento crítico,* no. 21 (1968), p. 116.
3. *Der Spiegel,* no. 51 (1967).

Appendix

Che's Reading

This is a partial and incomplete list of Che's reading, confined to works and writings referred to by Che himself, or that it is known for certain that he read.

World literature

Cervantes, *Don Quijote de la Mancha.* This pillar of Spanish culture had a great influence on the Cuban revolutionaries. Che read passages from it to his men in the Sierra Maestra.

Goethe, *Faust*
Mallarmé
Verlaine
Baudelaire
Alexandre Dumas
Jules Verne
Jack London, *Love of Life*
Robert Louis Stevenson
Emilio Salgari
Giovanni Papini, *Gog and magog*
(These were books Che read as a boy at home in Argentina.)
Julius Fučik, *Report from the Gallows*
Fadeyev, *The Young Guard*
(These works, inspired by Communism, were read in Mexico in 1954.)

Spanish-American literature

Alejo Carpentier, *El siglo de las luces (Explosion in a Cathedral)*
Léon-Felipe, *El Ciervo* (poems)

119

Benito Pérez Galdós

José Hernandez, *Martin Fierro* (*The Gaucho Martin Fierro*)

Jorge Icaza, *Huasipungo.* This book, which Che read in 1954, very probably had a great effect on him. It describes the brutal and inhuman exploitation of the Indian peasants by their landlords allied with imperialism, and their spontaneous revolt, drowned in blood. It may be that this work played the same role for Che as Balzac's *Les Paysans* did in the formation of Marx's ideas about the peasantry.

Pablo Neruda, *Canto General*

Enrique Rodó, *Ariel*

Marxism-Leninism

Marx, *Capital.* Che read this for the first time in Guatemala and Mexico in 1954–1955, when he was moving toward communism. He re-read it in 1963–1964, during the great economic discussion. He called it "a monument of the human mind," and based himself on it in his polemics against supporters of "market socialism."

Marx, *The Economic and Philosophic Manuscripts of 1844*

Marx, *The Poverty of Philosophy*

Marx, *Critique of the Gotha Programme*

It is probable, even though Che does not mention them explicitly, that he also read Marx's political writings: *The Communist Manifesto, The Eighteenth Brumaire of Louis Bonaparte,* and *The Civil War in France.*

Lenin, *State and Revolution*

Lenin, *Imperialism: The Highest Stage of Capitalism*

Lenin, *On the "United States of Europe" Slogan*

Lenin, *Problems of Building Socialism and Communism in the USSR.* In this collection Che was especially interested in Lenin's polemic with the Menshevik historian Sukhanov ("On Our Revolution," January 1923), which he regarded as highly relevant to the discussions that went on in Cuba.

Lenin, *The War Program of the Proletarian Revolution*

Trotsky, *History of the Russian Revolution*. This book was found by the Bolivian army in one of the guerrilla hiding places, and Che also mentions it in his diary (July 31, 1967). It is hard to see why he chose precisely this book rather than any other of Trotsky's: perhaps he considered the October Revolution, as a *proletarian insurrection*, significant in relation to the situation in Bolivia. It should be recalled that Debray, in his essay "Castroism: The Long March in Latin America," calls Bolivia the only country in Latin America where a workers' rising of the Soviet type is possible (in the mining areas). In his letter to the miners of Bolivia, Che refers to the role played by the mining proletariat, who will be able, thanks to the conditions created by the military development of the guerrilla struggle and its catalyzing political role, to deal that "single effective blow" under which "state power will crumble." However that may be, the fact that he carried this book with him into the Bolivian *maquis* shows the interest he was taking, in the last stage of his life, in the Bolshevik tradition in general, and Trotsky's ideas in particular.

Stalin, *Problems of Leninism*

Mao Tse-tung, *Writings on War*. Che read Mao in the Sierra Maestra in 1958, and it is certain, as he himself says, that he learned a lot from this. At the level of the strategy and tactics of guerrilla warfare, etc., the similarity of his ideas to Mao's is considerable. However, at the strictly "political" level, Che does not adopt certain classical Maoist analyses ("new democracy," "the bloc of four classes," etc.), precisely because his conception is that of the permanent revolution.

Giap, *People's War, People's Army*. In 1964 Guevara wrote an introduction to the Cuban edition of this book. Giap's work enabled him to enrich his theory of revolutionary war with the lessons of the Indochinese revolution: relations between army and people, role of the urban masses, role of the Leninist party, etc.

Otto Kuusinen, ed., *Fundamentals of Marxism-Leninism: A Manual*. A chapter of this book was published in Cuba in 1963, along with some speeches by Castro, under the title *El partido marxista-leninista*. Che wrote an introduction, which is one of the few documents in which he explicitly identifies himself with the Leninist theory of the party, "vanguard of the working class, leader of this class, able to show it the way to victory."

Latin America

Simon Bolívar

Fidel Castro

Jesús Silva Herzog. The experience of the Cardenas government in Mexico influenced Che, who read the writings of Silva Herzog in 1969, when he was preparing to expropriate the oil trusts in Cuba. Silva Herzog was the Mexican economist who drafted the law nationalizing the oil industry in Mexico in 1938.

Gabriel del Mazo, *Students and University Government*

José Martí. Like all the Cuban revolutionaries, Che held Martí in great veneration, and he especially appreciated his socialistic article on May Day and the workers' struggle in the United States.

Régis Debray, *Revolution in the Revolution?* Che appears to have made some criticisms of Debray's book, noted in the margins of his copy, which subsequently fell into the hands of the Bolivian army (*Bolivian Diary*, July 31, 1967).

Miscellaneous

Clausewitz, *On War*

M. Djilas, *The New Class*

E. Fischer, *The Necessity of Art*

Sigmund Freud

Frantz Fanon, *The Wretched of the Earth*. In 1965 Che planned to write an introduction to Fanon's book, which he had published in Cuba.

Marshal V. Sokolovsky, *Military Strategy*

Political economy

(Mostly read in connection with the economic debate of 1963-1964)

Academy of Sciences of the Soviet Union, *Textbook of Political Economy*

Paul Baran, *The Political Economy of Growth*

I. Ivonin, "The Combines (*kombinats*) of Soviet Enterprises," *Nuestra Industria*, no. 4

Oskar Lange, *Current Problems of Economic Science in Poland*

Ernest Mandel, *Marxist Economic Theory*

Victor Perlo, *The Empire of High Finance*

F. Tabeyev, "Economic Research and Management of the Economy," *Revue internationale* (no. 11), 1963.

Bibliography

Anthologies of Che's Writings

1. In Spanish

Cartas inéditas. Montevideo: Ediciónes Sandino, 1967.

Che. Havana: Instituto del Libro, 1969. Contains unpublished letters and documents of the period of guerrilla warfare in Cuba, together with the military articles Che published under a pseudonym in the journal of the Cuban revolutionary army, *Verde olivo.*

Obra revolucionaria. Mexico: Ediciónes Era, 1968. Has a very interesting introduction by R. F. Retamar, editor of the Cuban review *Casa de las Américas.*

Obras completas. Buenos Aires: Ediciónes de la Plata, 1968.

Pensamiento crítico, no. 9 (October 1967). A special issued devoted to Che.

2. In French

Oeuvres. Paris: Petite Collection Maspero, 1968. I: *Textes militaires;* II: *Souvenirs de la guerre révolutionnaire;* III: *Textes politiques;* IV: *Journal de Bolivie.* Volume I has the introduction by Retamar mentioned above. The collection brings together and completes Maspero's previous publication of Che's writings.

"Che" Guevara. Edited by J. J. Nattiez. Paris: Seghers, 1970. A very full political biography, with a selection of Guevara's writings.

3. In Italian

Opere. Milan: Feltrinelli, 1968–1969. I: *La guerra rivoluzionaria;* II: *Le scelte di una vera rivoluzione;* III: *Nella fucina del socialismo.*

Scritte, discorsi e diari de guerriglia (1959–1967). Turin: Einaudi, 1968.

4. In German

Brandstiftung oder Neuer Friede. Hamburg: Rowohlt, 1969. Introduction by Sven B. Papcke.

Che Guevara und die Revolution. Edited by H. R. Sonntag. Frankfurt: Fischer Bücherei, 1968. Writings by and about Che.

Che's Writings in English

Che Guevara on Guerrilla Warfare. Edited by Harries-Clichy Peterson. New York: Praeger, 1961.

Che Guevara on Revolution: A Documentary Overview. Edited by Jay Mallin. Miami: University of Miami Press, 1969.

Che Guevara Speaks. New York: Grove Press, 1969.

Che Guevara Speaks. Edited by George Lanvan. New York: Pathfinder, 1969.

Che: Selected Works of Ernesto Guevara. Edited by Rolando E. Bonachea and Nelson P. Valdés. Cambridge: M.I.T. Press, 1970. Contains the fullest bibliography of Che's writings.

Complete Bolivian Diaries of Che Guevara and Other Captured Documents. Edited by Daniel James. New York: Stein and Day, 1969.

Diary of Che Guevara. Edited by Robert Scheer. New York: Bantam, 1968.

Guerrilla Warfare. New York: Monthly Review Press, 1961.

Reminiscences of the Cuban Revolutionary War. New York: Monthly Review Press, 1968.

Venceremos! The Speeches and Writings of Che Guevara. Edited by John Gerassi. New York: Simon & Schuster, 1968.

Bibliography of Other Works Cited in the Text

Bettelheim, Charles. *La transition vers l'économie socialiste.* Paris: Maspero, 1968.

Debray, Régis. *Strategy for Revolution: Essays on Latin America.* New York: Monthly Review Press, 1970.

Fourier, Charles. *Théorie des Quatres Mouvements.* In *Morceaux choisis.* Paris: Editions Sociales, 1953.

Frank, Andre Gunder. *Capitalism and Underdevelopment in Latin America.* New York: Monthly Review Press, 1967.

——. *Latin America: Underdevelopment or Revolution?* New York: Monthly Review Press, 1969.

Franqui, Carlos. *The Twelve.* New York: Lyle Stuart, 1968.

Julien, Claude, ed. *Fidel Castro parle.* Paris: Maspero, 1961.

Kautsky, Karl. *Der Weg zur Macht.* 1910; 3rd ed. Berlin, 1920.

Lenin. *Works.* Moscow: Progress Publishers, n.d.

Lockwood, Lee. *Castro's Cuba, Cuba's Fidel.* New York: Vintage Books, 1969.

Lukács, Georg. *Frühschriften 1919-1922.* Neuwied: Luchterhand, 1968.

Mandel, Ernest. *The Formation of the Economic Thought of Karl Marx.* New York: Monthly Review Press, 1971.

Mariátegui, José Carlos. *Defensa de Marxismo.* Lima: Empresa Editora Amauta, 1964.

Marx, Karl. *Capital.* Vol. I. New York: International Publishers, 1967. Vols. II and III. Moscow: Progress Publishers, 1967.

——. *The Economic and Philosophic Manuscripts of 1844.* New York: International Publishers, 1964.

——. *The Poverty of Philosophy.* New York: International Publishers, 1963.

Marx, Karl, and Engels, Frederick. *Selected Works.* In three volumes. Moscow: Progress Publishers, 1969-1970.

——. *Marx and Engels on Religion.* Moscow: Progress Publishers, 1957.

Ponce, Aníbal. *Humanismo burgués y humanismo proletario.* Cuba: Imprenta Nacional, 1962; Mexico: Ediciónes Solidaridad, 1969.

Rojo, Ricardo. *My Friend Che.* New York: Grove Press, 1968.

Sinclair, Andrew. *Guevara.* New York: Viking Press, 1970.

Stalin, J. V. *The Economic Problems of Socialism in the USSR.* Moscow: Progress Publishers, 1952.